Popular Jewelry

1840-1940

Roseann Ettinger

Schiffer Publishing Ltd

Dedication

To my most precious jewels of all,
my children,
Amber and Clint.

Printed in China
ISBN: 0-7643-0133-0

Published by Schiffer Publishing, Ltd.
77 Lower Valley Road
Atglen, PA 19310
Phone: (610) 593-1777
Fax: (610) 593-2002
Please write for a free catalog.
This book may be purchased from the publisher.
Please include $2.95 for shipping.
Try your bookstore first.

We are interested in hearing from authors
with book ideas on related subjects.

Title page:
Dress clip made of gilded brass set with multi-colored glass stones, marked Czechoslovakia, circa 1930. $75-95.

Floridian Deco palm tree of base metal, enamel and rhinestones, circa 1930s. $35-50.

Flamingo brooch made of enameled base metal, circa 1930s. $35-45.

Opposite page:
Brooch of electroplated-base metal, enameled and rhinestone accents, marked Coro, circa 1940. $85-125.

Contents

Acknowledgments

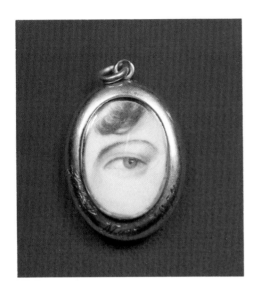

Hand-painted eye piece set in gold memorial pendant inscribed "KES" and dated May 1857. *Her Own Place.* $1600-1800.

My sincere thanks to my husband, Terry Ettinger, for tolerating my passion for collecting jewelry over the years and also for his help in the preliminary editing of the manuscript.

I would also like to thank my parents, Vito and Marie Rodino, for their never-ending support and constant encouragement with this project.

Appreciation to Matt Van Tassell for copy editing.

Special thanks to the following people for their advice and suggestions in the area of photography: Marc Anderson, Lynn Cairns, Gary Soult, Steve Soult and Jeff Weidner from The Big Picture Company, Mt. Laurel, New Jersey; Glenn Hunt, Tom Kirk and Josiah Reed Jr. from The Camera Shop, Burlington, New Jersey; Everett Turner from Mount Holly Camera Center, Mt. Holly, New Jersey; Greg Leomparra from Optica Inc., Cinnaminson, New Jersey; Billy Rogers from The Photo Shop, Mt. Holly, New Jersey; Doug Congdon-Martin from Schiffer Publishing; and Nancy Wegard, Willingboro, New Jersey.

I would also like to thank the following people for allowing me to photograph some of their wonderful jewelry: Marceline Lotman and George Wurtzel from Her Own Place, Moorestown, New Jersey; and Lenore and Larry Katz from Past to Present, Asbury Park, New Jersey; Marie Rodino; and Heidi Peinsipp Tomasello.

Large square painted porcelain brooch in twisted brass frame done in the Neoclassical style signed Angelica Kauffman, circa early 1800s. $235-275.

Preface

Collecting antique jewelry can bring you endless hours of enjoyment, for it not only satisfies a love of days gone by but also brings a yearning to learn more about other times and places. The collector shows a desire to be unique in setting, rather than following, fashion trends. For some, this passion can blossom into business for it is a treasure hunt and the fun never seems to end. Even today, the variety of what is available is immeasurable.

Over ten years ago an accidental sequence of events introduced me to the joys of being a collector. Attending an estate sale one morning my attention was drawn to a little wicker sewing basket. I opened it to see what was inside. Among the spools of thread, old packages of needles and assortment of thimbles, I noticed what appeared to be a piece of jewelry at the bottom of the basket. It was entangled in threads that had undoubtedly surrounded it for years. I gently pulled it out and immediately became entranced by the uniqueness of what appeared to be an Egyptian-style necklace. I examined it closely, wondering if I should buy it. Thinking I would never wear it, I finally put it back. I browsed a little longer but my thoughts kept returning to the necklace. I was beginning to think it was so unusual I shouldn't pass it up. I went back to look again. Luckily it was still there and I bought it. How could I go wrong for a dollar? Maybe I would wear it. Arriving home, I tried on the necklace. I wondered who originally owned it. What was the occasion to buy such a dynamic piece of jewelry? I only wished it could talk.

A few weeks later, I went to a huge indoor antique market. A little shop nestled in the back of the large building was crammed full of antique jewelry. As I entered this shop, one showcase caught my eye. A mate to my Egyptian-style necklace encircled a black velvet neck form. However, this one had a bracelet and earrings to match. What was so special about this set that it commanded the center of attention in the most prominent showcase? As I gazed at it, a woman approached and asked if I needed assistance. I inquired about the prominently displayed set. She said the necklace was styled to resemble the artifacts discovered in the excavation of King Tutankhamen's tomb in the 1920s. It was made of coral and turquoise beads set in brass filigree. The set retailed for $200. I'd expected the price to be around $25. I was stunned! My initial expectation had increased greatly, but not nearly as much as my appreciation for antique jewelry. From that moment I wanted to learn all I could about these fascinating items. The search was on.

Ten years later, the search is still on. Now there is more competition. Prices have risen, but the lure and curiosity keep the pace going. Men and women of all ages crowd jewelry tables at flea

Brooch, in the shape of a hand holding a flower bouquet, made of a hand-painted composition, circa 1875. $85-100.

Brooch made of gold electroplated base metal marked Coro; 1935-40. $50-65.

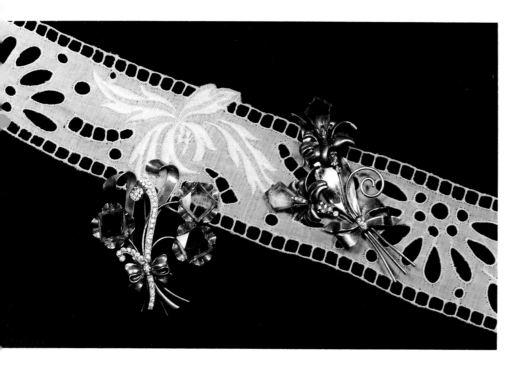

Two sterling floral sprays with rhinestone ornamentation and beautifully-cut topaz-colored glass stones, circa 1940s. $150-200 each.

Beautifully made necklace of brass and simulated amethyst stones and drops with leaf ornamentation, circa 1870. $275-300.

markets, antique shows and estate sales. Auction houses are beginning to specialize in estate jewelry sales. Designer fashion jewelry of the early twentieth century is selling for extremely high prices. Georgian jewelry is usually seen only in museums, and early Victorian jewelry is priced well above what the novice and intermediate collector can afford to pay; but jewelry made after 1850 is more modestly available. Antique jewelry has become so popular that some of the best department stores on Fifth Avenue in New York City have showcases filled with antique and period jewelry as well as fine and costume jewelry.

Because of rising values, reproductions of antique jewelry abound. The growing popularity has prompted imitators to reproduce period jewelry, especially that of the Art Nouveau and Art Deco designs. Most advanced collectors have acquired the ability to recognize reproductions. If you are a beginner in the field, ask plenty of questions. Some dealers use a sales pitch and will tell you anything in order to make a sale. If a piece of Art Nouveau style jewelry looks like it has just been cast, it probably has. If the marcasites in the Art Deco ring you want to buy are glued in, the ring is probably new. If a dealer says that the nineteenth-century brooch she is trying to sell you belonged to her grandmother, check the clasp; if it is a safety clasp, it is probably not Victorian. Safety catches were introduced in the second decade of the twentieth century. If the reproductions are what you want, then by all means buy them, but don't be fooled into believing they are authentic!

As you go through the following pages, we hope the excitement of seeing and learning gives you as much pleasure as it has given me over the years.

Roseann Ettinger
Mount Holly, New Jersey
October 1989

Introduction

During the Industrial Revolution of the nineteenth century, factories began mass-producing jewelry. Machine stamping and electroplating were invented and materials other than gold were used in jewelry manufacture. These new and exciting processes were incorporated with previous methods of imitating precious stones, enabling lovely imitation jewels to be mass-produced. Thereafter, prices for individual pieces came down to fractions of the costs of a generation earlier. Working class people were able to purchase jewelry which no longer was a luxury only the elite could afford. As a result, more jewelry was manufactured, purchased, worn and kept for posterity.

This book is intended to aid the reader in identifying period jewelry. While much of the jewelry pictured dates from the turn of the century to World War II, many pieces dating from the mid-to-late 1800s are also included to note style changes and characteristic trends and influences of nineteenth-century designs. In order to understand what was happening in jewelry design at the turn of the century, one must be aware of the cultural and artistic changes that occurred in both Europe and America in the late 1800s. Styles and characteristics overlapped from one period to the next. Individual designers and schools of design used re-occurring themes. Once these trends and influences are recognized, identification will become easier.

The jewelry discussed herein is categorized as Victorian, Art Nouveau, Edwardian, Transitional, and Art Deco. **Victorian** jewelry was produced during the reign of England's Queen Victoria from 1837 to 1901. **Edwardian** refers to the jewelry made during the reign of England's King Edward VII from 1901 until 1910. **Art Nouveau** encompasses the free-flowing style made from 1895 until 1914; and finally, **Art Deco** was the geometric style that flourished between World War I and World War II. During the transition from Art Nouveau (or "new art") to Art Deco (or "modern art"), some jewelry made in Austria and that made in Czechoslovakia had a unique style that this author feels should not be "solely" classified as Art Nouveau or Art Deco. For clarity, this jewelry, made prior to the 1925 Paris Exhibition, will be termed **Transitional**. It is often difficult for the collector to distinguish between late Art Nouveau and early Art Deco. Being able to recognize that a piece of jewelry is transitional clearly aids the collector in dating the piece more accurately.

Celtic-type brooch hallmarked sterling, circa 1885. $50-75.

Hollow cross made of gilded brass and set with brilliant, circa 1875. $125-150.

Victorian	1837-1901	Transitional	1910-1925
Art Nouveau	1895-1914	Art Deco	1910-1930
Edwardian	1901-1910	Other trends and influences	1930-1940

Antique jewelry is "wearable art" and should be appreciated as such. The jewelry worn by our ancestors was made with skill and a genuine love of the craft. Although most of the jewelry pictured in this book was not unique, the quality of details and workmanship may be superior to the mass-produced jewelry of today. The designers and craftsmen of yesteryear were very imaginative and cared deeply about the forms they created, whether hand-crafted or machine-made. To be a collector of wearable heirlooms in the late-twentieth century is to be appreciative of the imaginations of the craftsmen who created them.

2. HANDSOME SET OF SOLID 14 karat gold Brooch and Earrings, having a genuine coral rose mounted in the centre ; complete set, $8.75.

5. VERY RICH SET OF SOLID 14 karat gold, beautifully trimmed with green frosted gold leaves, massive in design, $20.50.

8. A NEW DESIGN OF SOLID GOLD EARRINGS after a Grecian pattern, very fashionable, $4.50.

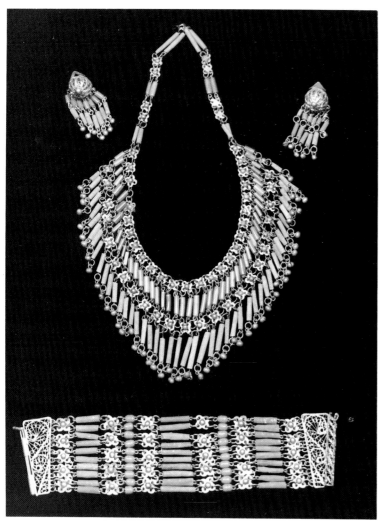

Parure consisting of fringed necklace, bracelet and earrings made of brass filigree, coral and turquoise in the Egyptian style, circa 1925-1930. $450-500.

Jewelry made of solid gold and rolled gold plate featured in *Ehrichs Fashion Quarterly* of 1879.

Chapter One

Victorian

The nineteenth century was a lavish mixture of previous styles: Renaissance, Gothic, Baroque, Greek and Etruscan designs were incorporated in jewelry manufacture. The prominent designers such as Froment-Meurice in France, Castellani in Italy and Giuliano in England were influenced by nature, artistic developments and archaeological excavations. The development and refinement of paste in the previous century was used extensively for imitating diamonds and other precious stones. Pinchbeck had also been utilized as a good substitute for gold. A tremendous amount of imitation jewelry was made of pinchbeck and set with paste stones.

Cut steel

Cut steel jewelry was fashionable in Europe during the latter part of the eighteenth century and continued to be so well into the nineteenth century. It had a dual purpose: it was used as a substitute for metals as well as for diamonds. The more facets the cut steel had, the more brilliant it became when light reflected from the facets. Genuine cut steel is always riveted to a metal background.

Marcasites (which are iron pyrites, sometimes called Fool's Gold) are sometimes mistaken for cut steel. Set just like stones, they were also being used as substitutes for diamonds.

The cut steel industry flourished in making shoe buckles prior to 1800 when shoe laces were introduced. Afterwards, chatelaines, clasps, brooches, earrings, necklaces, buttons and even tiaras and hair combs were made from cut steel. Genuine cut steel was also imitated; stamped out rosettes, similar in appearance to the actual steel facets, were made out of thin sheets of steel and sometimes tin.

In England, the coronation of Queen Victoria in 1837 began the historical era known as *the Victorian period*. With the British Empire acquiring this young woman as its monarch, there was a renewed interest in jewelry. Victoria's passion for jewelry sparked a general curiosity in old styles and she created new styles of her own. She was especially fond of snake jewelry; a theme which is seen throughout the entire 64 years of her reign. Since women generally wanted to emulate the Queen, they had rings, brooches, bracelets and necklaces fashioned into slithering serpents and sometimes garnished with stones.

No. 186. $15 00

Gold cross advertised in *BHA Illustrated Catalogue* of 1895.

Hollow brooch and two crosses made of rolled gold plate, circa 1875-1895. $95-150 each.

No. 207. Each, $7 00
Engraved.

No. 208. Each, $5 50
Enameled.

Engraved and enameled crosses made of 14k gold, circa 1895.

In the middle of the nineteenth century, the benefits of the Industrial Revolution were felt in all parts of society worldwide. Electroplating had been developed early in the nineteenth century and by 1840, for example, the Birmingham firm of Elkington applied this new process to jewelry manufacture. This allowed for tremendous amounts of jewelry to be made at much lower prices. Birmingham became the center of mass-produced jewelry in England. Small family-run businesses and cottage crafts were being replaced by large factories. The factories began mass-producing jewelry and accessories, enabling the working person to own what they once only dreamed about. Jewelry was no longer just for the elite and nobility. More jewelry was manufactured, purchased, worn and eventually passed down through the years. The beginnings of costume jewelry go as far back as the developments of paste, pinchbeck and cut steel, but only with industrialization and mass production in the middle of the nineteenth century could costume jewelry begin to flourish.

Department Stores

With this new industrial growth in Europe and America, the emergence of a new class of people became evident: people with buying power. This power eventually led to the evolution of department stores. *Bon Marche'*, for example, opened its doors in Paris in 1838. It started out as a small shop selling a variety of goods at low prices. By the 1850s it had grown and began to resemble what we today call a department store. In 1861, John Wanamaker founded his first department store in Philadelphia. Knowing that women always looked to Paris for new fashion trends, Wanamaker proudly presented Paris fashions in America. Strawbridge and Clothier opened in 1868, also in Philadelphia, and Bloomingdales in New York City opened in 1872. Liberty and Company, founded by Sir Arthur Lasenby Liberty, opened on Regent Street in London in 1875. Liberty catered to the "avant garde" society and carried vast amounts of Japanese and Indian goods. Liberty played an important role in the Art Nouveau movement which was germinating at this time.

Mail orders

Mail-order business then became big. Aaron Montgomery Ward, founder of Montgomery Ward and Company, started his mail-order business in 1872. In that same year, Wanamaker began selling his goods by mail. R.H. Macy jumped on the band wagon in 1874. Mail order already had become very competitive by that time.

Young Richard Sears began his career selling watches, and in 1886 founded the R.W. Sears Watch Company in Minneapolis. Business went so well for him that he moved to Chicago and advertised for a watchmaker to help out with his newly found business. Sears needed help in this venture since he did not know a thing about watches or their internal mechanisms. Alvah Curtis Roebuck answered the ad and Sears gladly gave him the job. In 1893, the business became Sears, Roebuck and Company.

Mail-order catalogs provided the means of learning current fashion trends as well as allowing the consumers to order anything their hearts desired without ever having to leave home. Offering competitive prices and a convenient way to shop was the key to their success. The catalogs were treasured and served as "Wish Books" to be thoroughly enjoyed.

Crystal Palace

On May 1, 1851, The Crystal Palace Exhibition took place in London at Hyde Park. Prince Albert played an important part in getting the exhibition underway. Queen Victoria presided over the opening ceremonies wearing a pink and silver gown and the Koh-i-Noor diamond. The Royal Family frequented the exhibit many times. This spectacular event, which lasted almost six months, was an immense assemblage of arts and industries of the world. Craftsmen and artisans displayed a wealth of goods; some unique to the times and some influenced by other times and places. Nature was a common theme seen in jewelry design as well as furniture, glassware, metalware and textiles. Celtic jewelry from Ireland was displayed along with chatelaines made from cut steel. The year of the Crystal Palace Exhibition was a very happy one for Queen Victoria. It marked the midway point in her marriage to Albert. Ten years later, however, the mood would change.

Black Jewlery

In 1861, both Queen Victoria's mother and her husband, Albert, died. The Queen became obsessed with her mourning and it generated the popular fashion during the rest of her life. As a result, black jewelry and clothes became fashionable. Mined in Whitby, England, jet is an opaque black fossil of wood or hard coal which had been known of since ancient times. Early in the nineteenth century, jet jewelry sales were slow. However, by the 1870s, the industry had skyrocketed. Workshops were scattered throughout Whitby and fashion magazines and catalogs were promoting the sale of jet jewelry and hair ornaments. Jet articles became a very important industry due to the dramatic length of time that Victoria mourned for Albert. Jet was a very soft substance which enabled the craftsman to carve and engrave without much difficulty. It also takes a high polish. Not all jet was polished, some of it was made with a dull matte finish. Jet is very light in weight and massive pieces of jewelry were fashioned from this material. In the United States, too, at the time of the Civil War, people commemorated the deaths of their loved ones by wearing black jewelry.

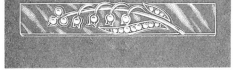

No. 2650. Real Onyx.............Each, $8 00
18 Real Pearls.

Black onyx and seed pearl brooch, circa 1895.

Fob chain, 24 inches long, made of small jet beads with a matte-finish, strung on a gold filled chain with a small round hand-engraved initial fob attached to a gold filled hook. $175-225. / Brooch in the shape of a heart made of French jet. $50-65. / Hand carved jet brooch with flower ornamentation, circa 1875-1890. $120-140.

Real Onyx...........Each, $11 00
Real Whole Pearl.

Imitation Onyx......Each, $11 00
Drops to Match.......Pair, 11 00

Real and imitation onyx featured in *BHA Illustrated Catalogue* of 1895.

BLACK ONYX BROOCHES AND PINS.

Fine Polished Rolled Plate Mountings.

No. 2835. Each............$1 50
Matted, Jet Stem.

No. 2836. Each............$1 75
Crape Finish.

No. 2837. Each............$1 25
Matted, Jet Stem.

No. 2838. Each............$0 92
Matted Finish.

No. 2839. Each............$1 60
Matted, Jet Stem.

No. 2840. Each............$1 50
Crape Finish.

No. 2841. Each............$1 75
Crape Finish.

No. 2842. Each............$1 50
Matted Finish.

No. 2843. Matted, Real Pearl..Dozen, $13 50

No. 2844. Crape Finish........Dozen, $8 00

No. 2845. Matted and Polished..Dozen, $10 00

Assortment of black onyx brooches pictured in the BHA Illustrated Catalog of 1895.

Vest chain made of jet beads and gold-plated findings. $85-125. / Two bar pins made of black onyx, gold and seed pearls. $100-150 each. / Watch pin made of black enameled base metal with retractable reel hook, marked American Optical Company, circa 1880-1900. $65-85.

Variety of black enameled bar pins, circa 1880-1900. The pin at the bottom has genuine cut steel riveted to form a frame. $25-75 each.

French jet choker and bracelet, circa 1890. $75-150.

By the 1880s, new materials were being used in place of jet. The most popular was "French Jet" which was actually black glass. Bohemian glass artisans produced enormous quantities of black glass for use in jewelry manufacture. In Ireland bog oak, which was a dark brown peat-like substance, resembling wood, was utilized. Gutta-percha, a natural brownish-black rubbery substance, had also proven to be a good substitute for jet. Gutta-percha was molded while bog oak was usually carved. Irish shamrocks, for example, were often carved on bog oak jewelry. Tortoiseshell also was used as well as black onyx and black enamel. Those of a more affluent background wore black pearls.

Clasp made of molded gutta percha, circa 1885. $135-165.

In 1880, *Ehrichs' Fashion Quarterly* pictured a bracelet made of four bands of black rubber combined with real jet ornamentation selling for $.39 per pair. In 1882, *Ridleys' Fashion Magazine* displayed a variety of hair ornaments also made from black rubber, as yet another substitute for jet. Black rubber was sometimes called vulcanite or ebonite. Bracelets made from dulled rubber balls, stating they were "equal in appearance to jet" sold for $.50 per pair. Real jet hair ornaments in this same magazine sold for $.25 and wide hair combs sold for $.75.

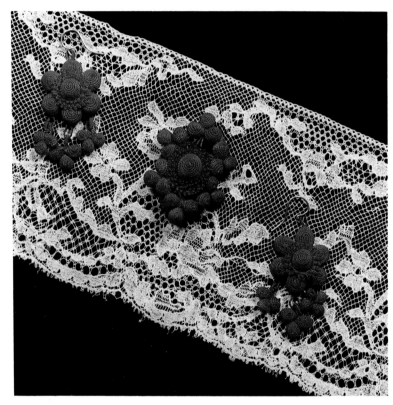

Brooch made of 9K gold set with three rows of faceted Bohemian garnets and human hair under a panel of glass, circa 1880. *Her Own Place.* $275-300.

Gold filled locket containing human hair under glass panel, circa 1885. $150-200.

Brooch and pierced earrings made of dyed horse hair, circa 1880. *Her Own Place.* $200-250.

Hairwork jewelry offered for sale in 1862 as pictured and priced in *Godey's Lady's Book.*

HAIR ORNAMENTS.

Ladies wishing hair made into Bracelets, Pins (which are very beautiful), Necklaces, or Ear-rings, can be accommodated by our Fashion Editor. A very large number of orders have recently been filled, and the articles have given great satisfaction.

We give the prices at which we will send these beautiful articles:—

Breastpins, from $4 to $12.
Bracelets, from $3 to $15.
Necklaces, from $6 to $15.
Hair Studs from $5 50 to $11 the set.
Ear-rings, from $4 50 to $10.
Rings, from $1 50 to $3.
Fob-chains, from $6 to $12.
Sleeve Buttons from $6 50 to $11 the set.
The Charms of Faith, Hope, and Charity, $4 50.

HAIR is at once the most delicate and lasting of our materials, and survives us like love. It is so light, so gentle, so escaping from the idea of death, that, with a lock of hair belonging to a child or friend, we may almost look up to heaven and compare notes with the angelic nature—may almost say: "I have a piece of thee here, not unworthy of thy being now."

1-10 GOLD EXTRA QUALITY HAIR MOUNTS.

These Mountings, including Bar, Toggle and Swivel, are made of a finer quality and extra thickness of Rolled Gold Plate.
Are well finished and have the appearance of an expensive gold mount.   Hard Solder.

 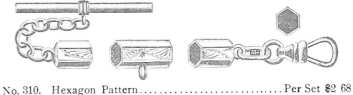

No. 309.   Fluted Pattern...............................Per Set $2 68   No. 310.   Hexagon Pattern.............................Per Set $2 68

SOLID GOLD HAIR MOUNTS.

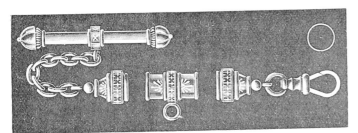 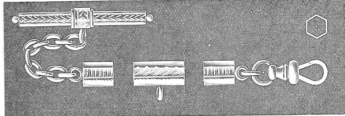

No. 300.   Round, Chased............................Per Set $8 50   No. 304.   Hexagon, Chased.................... .....Per Set $ 8 00
No. 301.   Center and Tips Separate...................   "   3 00   No. 305.   Double Mounting for Two Strands........ "   10 50

Hair jewelry

People at the end of the nineteenth century commonly were very sentimental. So influential, Queen Victoria's passion for sentimental or "commemorative" jewelry helped popularize jewelry made from human hair. The hair of a deceased loved one would be artistically arranged in delicate designs or sentimental scenes, which would then be retained under a panel of glass. Rings, brooches, lockets and pendants were made in this manner. Later in the century, hair itself made up the jewelry. This form was called "hair work" and became popular in the mid 1800s. Hair was braided or woven into intricate patterns. The pieces, cut in desired lengths, were fitted with solid gold, or gold-plated mountings. Necklaces, bracelets and especially watch chains were made of hair and were extremely fashionable. Hair also took the form of hollow brooches, crosses and earrings. Occasionally, horse hair was employed, especially for the beginner, since it was coarser and easier to work.

Hair work

Americans were enlightened about this unusual craft by means of *Godey's Lady's Book* in the 1850s. In each issue, instructions were given for different types of hair work jewelry. The women of this period would spend hours preparing the hair and then doing the braiding required for their specific patterns. When the work was completed it was sent to a jeweler for fittings. Many fine pieces of sentimental jewelry were made in the second half of the nineteenth century using this medium. The Civil War was partially responsible for the enormous popularity of hair jewelry in the United States. However, by the end of the century, hair jewelry had lost its appeal. Shortly after the death of Queen Victoria in 1901, it became a lost art form.

Hair mountings for watch chains made of solid gold and rolled gold plate, circa 1895.

Hairwork watch chain with gold filled mountings accented with rubies, circa 1865-1885. $150-200.

Cameos

Inasmuch as the people were sentimental, they were also romantics and loved to travel. Purchasing a piece of jewelry on their travels was customary. When in Italy, cameos were purchased. Early cameos were carved from carnelian, agate, sardonyx, lava and black onyx. Later, shell was used as well as coral, jet and rock crystal. Lava from Pompeii was expertly carved in classical heads, usually in high relief. German artists produced lovely porcelain and glass cameos. Again, Queen Victoria's apparent interest in cameos inspired craftsmen throughout England and workshops opened, especially in Birmingham, completely devoted to carving cameos. A distinct Victorian innovation was the cameo *habille'*, in which the woman in the cameo wears a piece of jewelry; most of the time it is a diamond pendant.

To determine a cameo that is superior, check the carving very closely. The ones with smooth, elegant and flowing lines, incorporated with very detailed clothing and sometimes flowers in the hair are worth much more than their counterparts with sharp, harsh and rigid lines.

Cameo *habillé* made of 14K white gold filigree with diamond mounted in beautiful carved shell cameo, circa 1890-1910. $725-850.

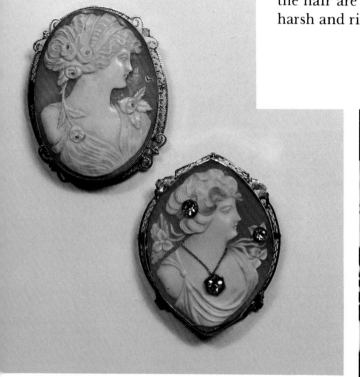

Handmade cameo pendant necklace made of lava, carved in high relief, set in brass, circa 1860. $350-425.

Carved shell cameo set in 14K gold frame. $600-650. / Cameo *habillé* set in 14K gold frame with three diamonds mounted in carved shell cameo, circa 1890-1910. $825-875.

Mosaics

Another type of souvenir jewelry termed "archaeological," made popular after the excavations of Pompeii and Herculaneum, was mosaic jewelry. Mosaics made especially in Florence were known as *pietra dura*. They were constructed of small pieces of stone such as malachite, lapis lazuli, coral, opal and others skillfully arranged into a black background, usually of marble. The themes for design were primarily floral and they became miniature works of art. Another style of mosaics, Roman or Byzantine, were made of tiny pieces of cut glass creating detailed landscapes, flowers and classical temples. Mosaics of superior quality were mounted in solid gold frames; sometimes pinchbeck and sterling silver was used. Those pieces of a lesser quality were set in gold-filled or brass mountings. Mosaics were popular in England between 1820 and 1860. Those that were made in England were not as elaborate as the Italian mosaics, but still were very desirable. Even today, mosaics are produced in Italy for tourists.

Roman mosaic picture frame made of gilded brass marked Italy, circa 1880-1890. $75-100.

Roman or Byzantine mosaic earrings in silver frames. *Her Own Place.* $125-175.

Pietra dura or Florentine mosaic brooch with gold frame. $400-450. / *Pietra dura* mosaic brooch in silver frame, English, circa 1860. $200-250. English mosaics were usually not as elaborate as the actual Italian mosaics but still very desirable. *Her Own Place.*

Pendant made of *pietra dura* mosaic set in 14K gold frame, circa 1860-1870. *Her Own Place.* $350-450.

Gilded brass and coral-colored Bohemian glass necklace, circa 1885. $100-135.

Coral

Coral was popular as a jewelry material from 1840 to 1870 when grand *parures* (complete sets of jewelry) were fashioned from this colorful underwater treasure. Coral, like jet, is relatively soft so it can be carved easily. Cameos, rings, brooches, bracelets and strands of polished beads were made in abundance, especially from the coral found in the waters of the Mediterranean. Children's jewelry, baby rattles and teething rings were also fashioned from coral since it was believed to ward off evil. It became a popular Christening present for this reason.

With the many motifs of nature found in jewelry design in the nineteenth century, coral took the form of flowers, twigs, branches and leaves. At times, this was somewhat easy to accomplish since coral in its natural state looks like little branches. This material was combined with intricate gold work and sometimes enamel. Coral comes in a variety of colors ranging from a very light pink to a deep blood red; the most popular being angel-skin pink.

Festoon necklace and pierced earrings made of gold and set with carved coral cameos in high relief, English, circa 1880. *Her Own Place.* $1600-1800.

Large pendant necklace made of brass and polished coral beads. / Small pendant necklace of brass and branch coral, circa 1875-1885. $75-100.

Agate and ivory

Besides cameos, mosaics and coral jewelry, there was also agate jewelry from Scotland and Celtic brooches from Ireland. Ivory and jade came from the Orient and silver and tiger-claw jewelry from India was very fashionable in the 1880s. Beautiful carved ivory jewelry could also be purchased from Germany and Switzerland.

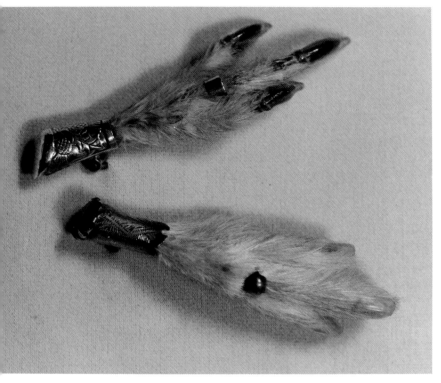

Two nineteenth-century Scottish brooches made of grouse feet with sterling silver ornamentation. The brooch at the bottom is set with a cairngorm, circa 1870. *Her Own Place.* $75-100 each.

Trio of Scottish pebble jewelry made of cairngorms, agate, jasper, bloodstone and gold, circa 1870-1880. *Her Own Place.* $125-150 each.

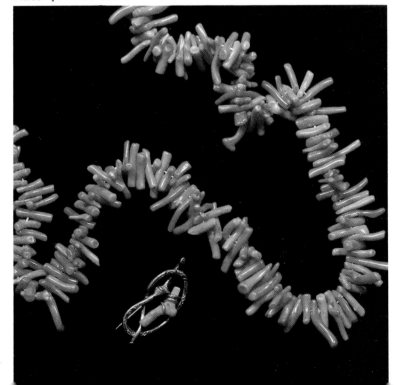

This 14K gold bracelet with three diamonds retailed for $112 in 1895.

22-inch strand of branch coral beads. $75-100. / Brooch made of rolled gold plate and branch coral, circa 1885-1895. $60-85.

Celluloid

Celluloid had been refined in 1868 by John Wesley Hyatt. This new man-made plastic could be made opaque, transparent or translucent in a variety of colors sometimes imitating ivory, tortoise-shell, coral, amber and jet. This revolutionary man-made material further encouraged designers and craftsmen to create unique jewelry. In addition, reproductions of original designs were made at affordable prices. Toilet articles were made of celluloid for many years imitating ivory. Celluloid was later found to be highly flammable and was eventually replaced by other man-made plastics.

Garnets

Garnets were often used in the eighteenth and nineteenth centuries. Most of the garnets that were employed in jewelry came from Mount Kozakov in Bohemia. The term "Bohemian Garnets" is used quite frequently when describing the garnet jewelry made during this era. After World War I, Bohemia became known as Czechoslovakia (More on this in Chapter IV).

Hair pin in celluloid with ornamental gilded brass top. / Hair pin in celluloid with aluminum top set with brilliants, circa 1895-1910. $65-95 each.

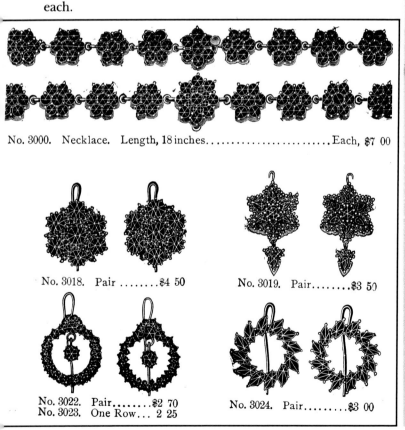

No. 3000. Necklace. Length, 18 inches.........................Each, $7 00

No. 3018. Pair $4 50

No. 3019. Pair........$3 50

No. 3022. Pair........$2 70
No. 3023. One Row... 2 25

No. 3024. Pair........$3 00

Bohemian garnet necklaces and ear drops, circa 1895.

Bohemian garnet necklace and brooch in gilded silver, circa 1890-1895. Necklace $650-795. Brooch $125-150.

The jewelry of the third quarter of the nineteenth century was rather large in size. Everything appeared to dangle and it seemed that this ostentatious style was widely accepted. Jewelry was also very colorful at this time. Gemstones such as amethysts, garnets and peridots were employed as well as ivory, coral, amber and jet. Different enameling techniques were utilized and a popular look was dark blue enamel on gold. Necklaces were in vogue primarily due to the low necklines in popular evening wear. Earrings were very large and sometimes hung to the shoulders. Brooches were worn occasionally in conjunction with necklaces and huge lockets. It was not unusual for a woman to be seen wearing a necklace, a locket, three or more bracelets, a brooch, earrings and a few finger rings all at the same time. Jewelry was the height of fashion!

Pendant necklace made of brass with cabochon-cut pink glass stones set in flower motif. / Fringed necklace made of brass, circa 1875-1885. $85-150 each.

Pendant made of brass and set with multi-colored glass stones. Originally, this pendant was half of a clasp. $85-100.

Large diamond-shaped brass filigree brooch set with multi-colored glass stones, circa 1875. $125-150.

Necklaces

Necklaces, chokers, lockets and long chains were in vogue throughout the late nineteenth century. Necklets, which were longer than chokers but shorter than the necklace we know today, were popular in the early period. Long ribbon necklaces or pearls with tassels, both termed *sautoirs*, were worn throughout the nineteenth century. Festoon necklaces, which make a lace-like pattern usually produced by a series of chains, were fashionable in the late part of this era. Chokers and dog-collar necklaces along with fringed necklaces were also high fashion.

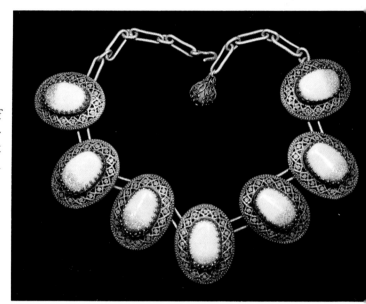

Fringed necklace made of brass and red cut glass drops, circa 1880-1885. $125-150.

Fringed necklace with very unusual shaped blue glass drops suspended from brass chain, circa 1870-1875. $250-300. / Brooch made of brass and Bohemian glass, circa 1905. $75-90.

Necklace made of German silver filigree medallions set with oval-shaped pink glass stones on heavy link chain, circa 1880s. $175-200.

Festoon necklace made of brass and topaz-colored glass stones, circa 1875-80. $250-300. / Brooch of gilded brass and glass, circa 1905-10. $65-80.

Necklace made of brass in openwork pattern and set with multi-colored paste stones, circa 1875-1885. $250-300.

Fringed necklace in brass, set with simulated amethyst stones, marbleized center stone and amethyst glass drops suspended from brass link chain, circa 1875-1880. $200-250.

Festoon necklace made of gilded brass and multi-colored glass drops, circa 1875. $250-300.

Necklace and brooch made of silver
filigree and green paste stones, circa
1885. $75-135 each.

Motifs from nature displayed in these
two pendant necklaces made of brass
and silver gilt, circa 1875-1885. $60-
85 each.

Silver-plated tassel necklace, circa
1880s. $75-95.

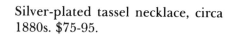

Fringed necklace made of brass with engraved links, filigree drops and clusters of Bohemian glass, circa 1875-1885. $75-100.

Choker made of brass mesh, circa 1865. $150-175.

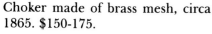

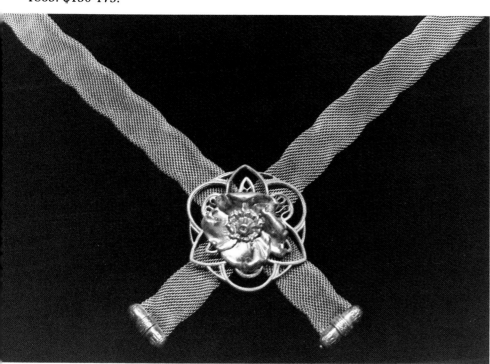

Bookchain necklace with detachable pendant brooch made of rolled gold plate with some pink and green gold ornamentation and a tiger eye cameo, circa 1885. / Bookchain necklace made of gilded brass with carnelian cameo, circa 1870-1880. $275-325 each.

Above from left:

Necklace of gilded brass with bezel-set simulated aquamarines accented with carved bone flowers, circa 1875-1885. $100-150.

Gothic-style cross made of silver and bezel-set simulated sapphires, marked Germany, circa 1885. $175-200.

Locket made of gilded brass and set with simulated pearls surrounding an opalescent center stone, circa 1875-1880. $100-125.

Necklace of gilded brass with oval hand-painted porcelain plaques and alternating rectangular segments accented with enamel, circa 1875-1880. $225-250.

Fringed necklace made of brass and pink glass stones, circa 1880-1890. $100-135.

Machine-stamped brass necklace set with purple and green glass stones, marked H. Pomerantz Inc. New York, circa 1880-1890. $100-135.

Lovely enameled locket in decorative brass mounting on large link chain, circa 1875. $140-160.

Bohemian glass and brass necklace, circa 1885-1890. $95-125.

No. 640. Pretty Silvered Daisy Pin. Price, 50c.

Silvered daisy pin offered for sale in 1879.

Flower necklet in silver gilt, circa 1880-1890. *Her Own Place.* $85-100.

Fringed necklace made of gilded brass filigree and blue glass drops, circa 1890. $135-175. /Brass and Bohemian glass screw-type earrings, circa 1910-1920. Transitional. $60-80.

Necklace, lace pin and stick pin all set with Fool's Gold (Iron Pyrite), circa 1890-1900. Necklace $125-175. Lace pin $35-50. Stick pin $45-75.

Bracelets

Bracelets were made very wide until the last quarter of the nineteenth century. They were usually sold in pairs and worn on each arm. Occasionally women wore them on the upper arm as well as at the wrist. Bracelets had been consistently stylish throughout the period. Cuff, multi-strand and link bracelets were made in abundance. Lacy filigree bracelets with detailed scrolling designs were made of polished silver, burnished gold, brass and gilt.

Two hinged bracelets made of brass, circa 1870-1880. $50-95 each.

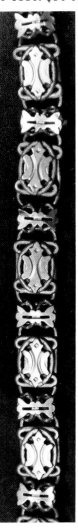

Link bracelet made of brass with gold ornamentation, circa 1860. $80-100.

Curb chain bracelet made of rolled gold plate with hand engraving on alternating links, circa 1895. $75-95.

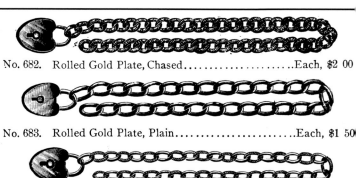

No. 682. Rolled Gold Plate, Chased.....................Each, $2 00

No. 683. Rolled Gold Plate, Plain.....................Each, $1 50

No. 695. Sterling Silver.................................Each, $1 50

No. 696. Sterling Silver, Plain.........................Each, $1 75

Curb chain bracelets made of rolled gold plate and sterling silver from 1895.

Hinged bracelet made of brass filigree and set with pink glass stones. / Cuff bracelet in silver with heart motif. / Bangle bracelet in brass with buckle closure, circa 1880-1890. $60-95 each.

Late Victorian bracelets from 1895.

No. 701. Rolled Gold Plate, Woven Wire, Best Quality......Per Pair, $5 00 Polished, Assorted Tips.

No. 702. Rolled Gold Plate, Assorted Patterns...............Per Pair, $5 00 Links Set with Ruby, Moonstone and other Color Sets.

Assorted Widths, Band.
No. 703. Rolled Plate, Best..Per Pair, $10 00
No. 704. Gold Filled   "   "   20 00

IMPORTED BOHEMIAN GARNET BRACELETS.

No. 705. Imported Bohemian Garnet Bracelet..Each, $9 00

No. 706. Imported Bohemian Garnet Bracelet...Each, $12 00

Brooches

Brooches were also made in great numbers using every type of material available to the craftsman or jeweler. New techniques as well as old were incorporated in producing brooches of exquisite quality and design. Tri-color gold brooches, usually in the form of flowers and leaves were made throughout the period. Malachite, turquoise, lapis lazuli and coral were employed along with garnets, amethysts and pearls. A considerable amount of real or imitation topaz was used and the mineral "tiger eye" was first used in jewelry manufacture in the 1880s. Bowknots, crescents, flower sprays, anchors, stars and hearts were desirable subjects. Buttercups and daisies, made in silver and gilt, often enameled in different colors, were favored motifs in the 1880s. Closer to the turn of the century, catalogs pictured lizard pins and stated they were the "latest in novelty jewelry." They were enameled and sometimes set with pearls, brilliants or cut steel. Although they appeared to be a novel idea, they had been worn in earlier decades. They were very similar to the lizard brooches manufactured today from sterling silver and marcasites. The girandole brooch was worn in the early period around 1840 to 1850, and the later period around 1880 produced scarf and bar pins made of gold, silver, oxidized brass, rolled gold plate and gilt. Hammered silver also created stylish designs at affordable prices. Black onyx, usually topped with gold and seed pearls, took the form of a bar pin and continued to be popular until the turn of the century.

Oval hand-painted porcelain brooch in brass frame, circa 1860-1870. $100-150.

Enameled and flower brooches from 1895.

Brooches and lace pins made of Mother of Pearl from 1895.

ENAMELED AND FLOWER BROOCHES.

Nos. 2804–5–6 are Enameled in Colors, with Shadings and Veins. The Enameling is as fine as on the very expensive Gold Goods. The others are Finest Rolled Plate.

No. 2804. Each............$3 75
Pansy in Colors.

No. 2805. Each............$4 25
Orchid in Colors.

No. 2806. Each............$4 00
Primrose in Colors.

No. 2822. Each............$1 25
Assorted Butterflies,
Roman and Polished.

MOTHER OF PEARL AND SEA SHELLS.

No. 2777. Each...$1 25
Pearl Crescent.

No. 2786. Each.....$1 13
Pearl Branch.

No. 2787. Each.............$0 63
Pearl Hand.

No. 2788. Each.............$1 12
Sea Shell.

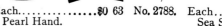

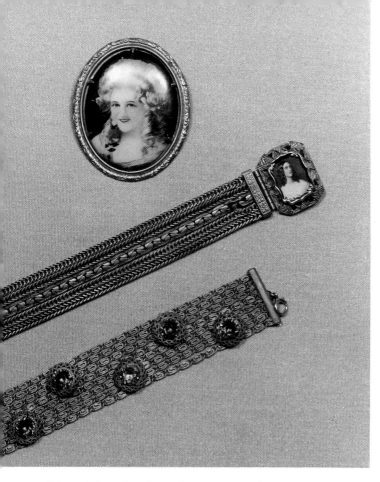

Sash pin made of brass with bezel-set blue glass stone and repoussé work, circa 1905. $100-150.

Celluloid cameo in brass frame. $75-95. / Two brass multi-strand link bracelets, circa 1875-1890. $75-100 each.

Daisy collar pin in brass with multi-colored enamel ornamentation, circa 1880. $45-65. / Bracelet in copper with enamel decoration, circa 1910. $50-75.

Three Victorian brooches made of rolled gold plate, some solid gold ornamentation, set with brilliants, circa 1875-1885. $75-125 each.

Sash pin made of brass and set with molded glass cameo, circa 1870-1875. $100-125.

Brooch, in the shape of a bunch of grapes, made of blue glass stones and gilded brass leaves, circa 1890. $100-135.

Engraved watch chatelette made of rolled gold plate, circa 1890. $50-75.

SOLID GOLD, GOLD FRONT, ROLLED PLATE CUFF OR BIB PINS.

No. 2957. Each, $2 00
Polished or Roman.

No. 2958. Each, $1 75
Polished or Roman.

No. 2959. Each, $1 75
Engraved.

No. 2960. Each, $2 00
Roman.

No. 2961. Each, $2 38
Enameled.

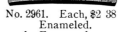

No. 2962. Each, $1 50
Roman, Engraved.

Above row is Solid Gold with Catches covering end of Pin. Plain Pins can be Engraved.

No. 2963. Pair, $1 50
Pet, Darling or Baby.

No. 2964. Pair, $1 50
Garnet Sets, Gold Front.

No. 2965. Pair, $1 50
Gold Front, Sets.

No. 2966. $12 00
Nos. 2966 to 2968 are Gold Front Style.

No. 2967. $12 00
Per Doz. Pairs.

No. 2968. $9 00
Engraved.

No. 2969. $3 50
Assorted.

No. 2970. $6 00
Chased.

No. 2971. $6 00
Chased.

No. 2972. $6 00
Chased.

No. 2973. $10 00
Enameled.

No. 2974. $10 00
Enameled.

Nos. 2969 to 2974, Prices Per Dozen Pairs.

Cuff and bib pins from 1895.

No. 2846. Each $2 25
Half Satin, Bright Engraved.

No. 2847. Each $2 25
Half Satin, Bright Engraved.

No. 2848. Each $2 25
Half Satin, Bright Engraved.

No. 2849. Each $2 00
Half Satin, Bright Engraved.

No. 2850. Each $1 75

No. 2851. Each $1 75

Late Victorian bar pins made with engraved gold fronts, circa 1895.

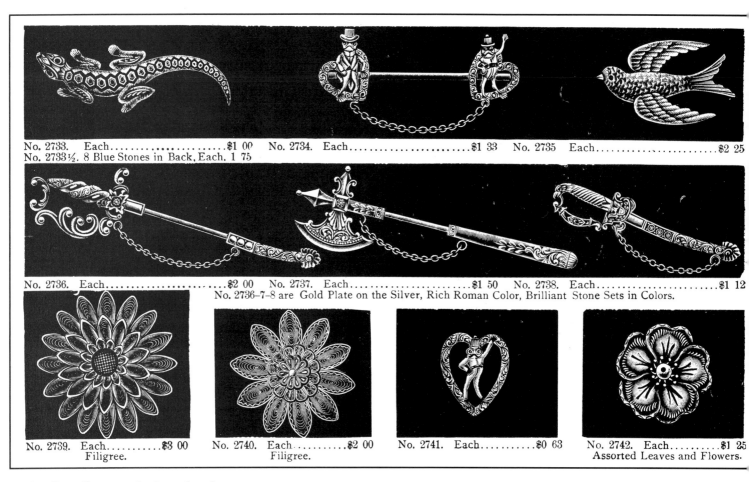

No. 2733. Each..................$1 00   No. 2734. Each....................$1 33   No. 2735 Each.....................$2 25
No. 2733½. 8 Blue Stones in Back, Each, 1 75

No. 2736. Each....................$2 00   No. 2737. Each....................$1 50   No. 2738. Each....................$1 12
No. 2736–7–8 are Gold Plate on the Silver, Rich Roman Color, Brilliant Stone Sets in Colors.

No. 2739. Each..........$3 00   No. 2740. Each.........$2 00   No. 2741. Each..........$0 63   No. 2742. Each.........$1 25
Filigree.   Filigree.   Assorted Leaves and Flowers.

Sterling silver novelty brooches from
1895.

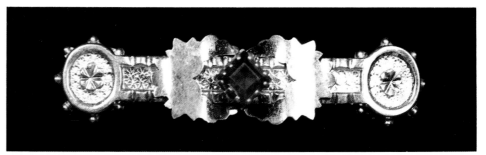

Bar pin in rolled gold plate set with
imitation ruby, circa 1880s. $85-110.

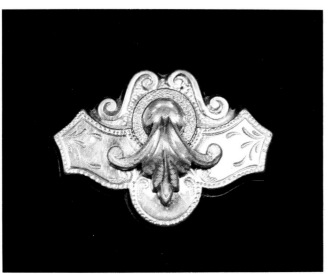

Hollow gold-plated brooch, circa
1895-1900. $70-90.

Earrings

Earrings were extremely popular throughout the late nineteenth century. The type and style of earring worn depended largely on the hair styles of the time. Earrings were made for pierced ears until the last decade of the century; at that time the screw-back was invented. Styles alternated from dangle to studs in a wide variety of materials. In the early period, the Creole earring was stylish. This type resembled our present-day hoop earring. In the later period, long drops and tassel earrings were worn. By 1880, pierced eardrops in the shapes of cones, hearts, leaves, daisies, fans and filigree balls were made of burnished gold, brass and gilt.

Assortment of late Victorian ear drops.

GOLD FRONT, ROLLED PLATE AND ONYX EAR DROPS.

PRICES PER DOZEN PAIRS.

Nos. 3239 to 3263, Hand Engraved Gold Fronts Soldered on Polished Rolled Plate Backs.   The best that are made.
Assorted Engravings in each number.

No. 3239. $14 00   No. 3240. $14 00   No. 3241. $14 00   No. 3242. $12 00   No. 3243. $12 00   No. 3244. $13 00   No. 3245. $13 00

No. 3267. Gold Wires, $7 50   No. 3269. Gold Wires, $6 50   No. 3271. Gold Wires, $9 00   No. 3273.   No. 3274.   No. 3275.   No. 3276.
No. 3268. Plate   "   5 00   No. 3270. Plate   "   4 00   No. 3272. Plain   "   8 00 $18 00 $15 00 $12 00 $11 00
Nos. 3273 to 3276, Finest 18 Karat Plate, Gold Ear Wires.   Warranted to Wear.

     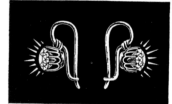

No. 3277. $18 00   No. 3278. $17 00   No. 3279. $12 00   No. 3280. $9 00   No. 3281. $7 00   No. 3282.   Dozen..........$9 00
Borneo, 1 C.   Borneo, ½ C.   Above row Imitation Diamonds.
No. 3283, Imitation Diamond Ear Drops, like Nos. 3281 and 3282, one Dozen Pairs in Satin Lined Box for $7.50.

No. 3284. $6 00   No. 3285. $6 00   No. 3286. $6 00   No. 3287. $12 00   No. 3288. $12 00   No. 3289. $12 00   No. 3290. $9 00
Sterling Silver,   Matted.   Polished.   Pearl Set.   Pearl Set.   Matted.
Turquoise Set.
Nos. 3285 to 3291 are Imitation Black Onyx, Rolled Plate Mountings.

No. 3291. $90 00   No. 3292. $84 00   No. 3293. $54 00   No. 3294. $24 00   No. 3295. $90 00   No. 3296. $24 00   No. 3297. $18 00
Assorted, Pearl Set.   Pearl Set.   Pearl Set Tops.   Polished.   Carved Leaf.   Matted.   Matted.
Nos. 3291 to 3297 are Real Black Onyx with Solid Gold Trimmings.

Buckles

Buckles were a necessary item throughout the nineteenth century. Shoe buckles were still made, even after the shoe lace had been introduced. Belt buckles, cloak and cape buckles were mass-produced. Buckles made prior to the 1850s were extremely ornate and garnished with precious stones. Buckles made after 1850, although still ornate, were made of oxidized silver, hammered base metal and sometimes celluloid. They were set with real gemstones or paste imitations. Cloak and cape buckles were usually called clasps and they became fashionable around 1860. They consisted of two identical halves that connected. The belt buckle at this time was usually made in one piece.

Very ornate sash buckle made of brass and set with cabochon-cut simulated turquoise stones, circa 1890. $125-150.

Three cloak clasps made of early plastics. The clasp in the center is carved Bakelite; the two on each end are made of celluloid, circa 1880-1910. $50-75 each.

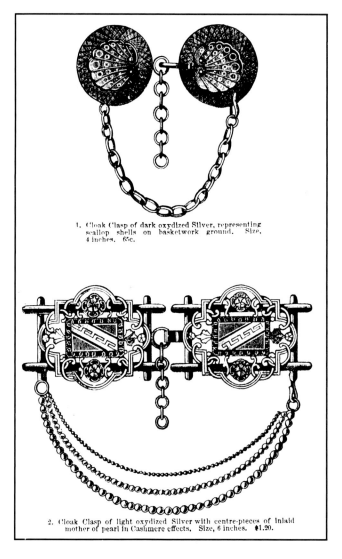

1. Cloak Clasp of dark oxydized Silver, representing scallop shells on basketwork ground. Size, 4 inches. 65c.

2. Cloak Clasp of light oxydized Silver with centre-pieces of inlaid mother of pearl in Cashmere effects. Size, 6 inches. $1.20.

Two cloak clasps made of oxidized silver as shown in *Ehrich 'Fashion Quarterly* of 1880.

No. 13. Belt Complete..Each, $8 50

No. 14. Belt Complete....................Each, $5 00

Ornate belt buckles of sterling silver from 1895.

Beautiful belt made of gunmetal and simulated amethyst stone, circa 1895-1900. $250-300.

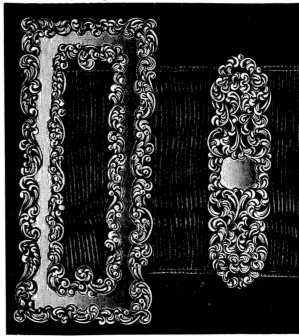

No. 16. Belt Complete....   .....Each, $5 34

No. 19. Belt Complete............................Each, $5 00

HAT PIN ASSORTMENT.

31192 Put up 3 dozen on small, neat and compact display stands, suitable for showcases and counters; the tops are finished in Roman and plain gold, enamel inlaid in colors, set in a complete assortment of brilliant cut stones of every description. All of the newest filigree patterns are included in this line. Per pad of 3 dozen pins..........1 95

Turn of the century hatpins.

Hatpins offered for sale from Lyon Brothers Catalog for 1899-1900.

Assortment of hatpins from the late nineteenth and early twentieth centuries. $25-50 each.

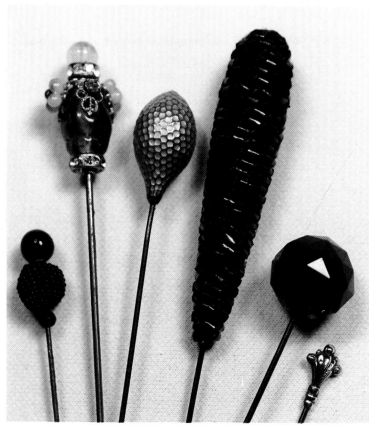

Hatpins

Hats were becoming very large in the late nineteenth century period and as a result hatpins became necessities. Some of the hatpins measured up to 12 inches in length. The shafts were usually made of steel, although other base metals in addition to solid gold and sterling silver were utilized. The hatpin heads were very decorative and fashioned in gold, sterling silver, ivory, porcelain, amber, jet and paste to name only a few. Because of the size of the hats, the hatpins began as functional items but became ornamental in time. They were even considered dangerous and guards were sold to cover the ends of pins that protruded from the hat.

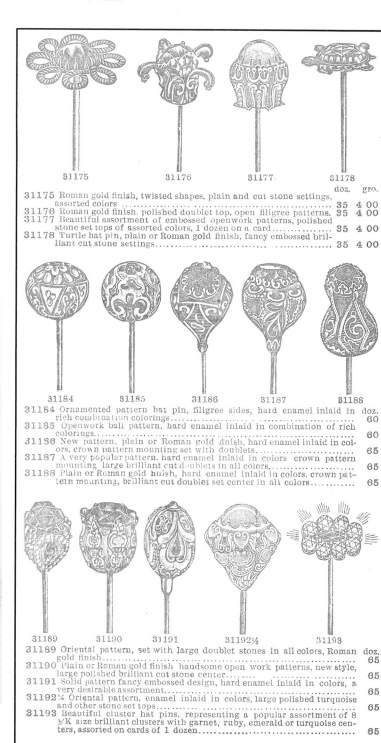

			doz.	gro.
31175 Roman gold finish, twisted shapes, plain and cut stone settings, assorted colors			35	4 00
31176 Roman gold finish, polished doublet top, open filigree patterns			35	4 00
31177 Beautiful assortment of embossed openwork patterns, polished stone set tops of assorted colors, 1 dozen on a card			35	4 00
31178 Turtle hat pin, plain or Roman gold finish, fancy embossed brilliant cut stone settings			35	4 00

		doz.
31184 Ornamented pattern bat pin, filigree sides, hard enamel inlaid in rich combination colorings		60
31185 Openwork ball pattern, hard enamel inlaid in combination of rich colorings		60
31186 New pattern, plain or Roman gold finish, hard enamel inlaid in colors, crown pattern mounting set with doublets		65
31187 A very popular pattern, hard enamel inlaid in colors crown pattern mounting large brilliant cut doublets in all colors		65
31188 Plain or Roman gold finish, hard enamel inlaid in colors, crown pattern mounting, brilliant cut doublet set center in all colors		65

		doz.
31189 Oriental pattern, set with large doublet stones in all colors, Roman gold finish		65
31190 Plain or Roman gold finish handsome open work patterns, new style, large polished brilliant cut stone center		65
31191 Solid pattern fancy embossed design, hard enamel inlaid in colors, a very desirable assortment		65
31192½ Oriental pattern, enamel inlaid in colors, large polished turquoise and other stone set tops		65
31193 Beautiful cluster hat pins, representing a popular assortment of 8 ⅜ K size brilliant clusters with garnet, ruby, emerald or turquoise centers, assorted on cards of 1 dozen		65

Hair combs

With the heightening of hair styles, hair combs were designed to fit the fashion picture. Treated with the same respect as jewelry, hair combs were made of some of the same materials. Decorative hair combs were not an innovation, they actually date back to ancient times but as early as the mid-1700s, farmers in New England began making decorative hair combs from ivory, horn and tortoiseshell. These combs were made by hand but after industrialization, machinery made the task easier. In the early nineteenth century, hair combs were fashioned from coral, cut steel and even special cast iron which was termed Berlin Ironwork; some of the combs were elaborately decorated with carved cameos. Classical influences such as Etruscan granulation, Renaissance *repousse'* and engraving, Gothic filigree and niello work were incorporated in the production of late nineteenth century hair ornaments. When Queen Victoria was given the title of Empress of India in 1876, beautiful ivory hair ornaments became the rage. During the many years of mourning for Prince Albert, jet, French jet, vulcanite and ebonite combs were stylish and abundantly made. Hair combs and hair pins were also made from celluloid which were good substitutes for tortoiseshell and ivory. These imitations were set with colored glass stones and they were sometimes carved and trimmed elaborately with gold and silver. Using celluloid lowered the price enabling more women to purchase hair ornaments.

No. 6452.   Each, $32 00
Heavy, 14 Karat.

No. 6456.   Each, $14 00
10 Karat Gold.

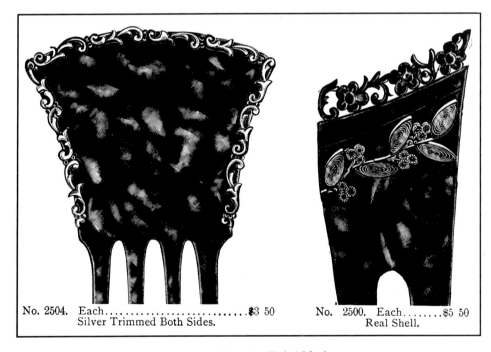

No. 2504.   Each.........................$3 50
Silver Trimmed Both Sides.

No. 2500.   Each.......$5 50
Real Shell.

Tortoiseshell and celluloid hair ornaments from 1895.

No. 6460.   Each, $7 50
10 Karat Gold.

Hair pins made of amber-colored celluloid with 10K and 14K gold tops.

No. 2510. Each..........$2 50
Trimmed Both Sides.

No. 2514. Each..............$2 00

No. 2518. Each........$1 92

Celluloid and tortoiseshell hair combs and hair pins trimmed in sterling silver from 1895.

Men's jewelry

The late nineteenth-century gentleman was also adorned with jewels. He wore pocket watches, watch chains, fobs and seals, tie pins, breast pins and signet rings. Collar studs were introduced before the middle of the century and cuff links appeared towards the end. Monocles, silver-topped walking canes, cigar cases and match safes were beautifully made and mass-produced. The variety of chains that were made was endless, especially towards the end of the century. Vest chains ranged from very plain to extremely ornate in hundreds of styles. Some were made of solid gold while others were made of silk grosgrain ribbon. Rolled gold plate, gold filled, brass and German silver were also used. Contrary to popular belief, German silver contains no silver whatsoever; it is actually an alloy of zinc, copper and nickel. German silver was also called "gunmetal" and used significantly in this period and into the early twentieth century. One very popular type of vest chain for men was called the "Albert" chain; its counterpart for women was called the "Victoria" chain. Still other chains were set with fancy intaglio cameos made of sardonyx or brown carnelian. The Lyon Brothers Catalog for 1899-1900 devoted 18 pages to men's chains alone. Prices ranged from 85 cents per dozen for fancy embossed curb chains with Roman gold finish to $15.50 for a solid ten-Karat gold chain with a diamond mounted in a Roman chased slide.

Above:
Match safe with repoussé work marked Silveroin, circa 1895. $80-100.

Opposite:
Match safes and stamp boxes in silver-plated nickel silver.

QUADRUPLE SILVER PLATED WARE.

MATCH BOXES.

BEST QUALITY, PLATED ON NICKEL SILVER. CUTS FULL SIZE.

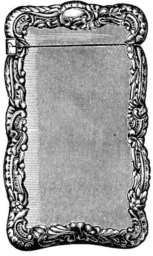

No. 984. [PUNITIVE]......$2 40   No. 873. [PUNSTER]......$2 40   No. 1001. [PURPORT].....$2 40   No. 950. [PURSUE]........$2 40

No. 865. [PURVEY].......$2 40   No. 981. [PUSTULE]......$2 40   No. 880. [PUSTULATE]....$2 40   No. 024. [PUTTOCK]......$1 50
                                                   Old Silver Finish with Counters.   Assorted Designs

POCKET STAMP BOXES.

BEST QUALITY SILVER PLATE ON NICKEL. CUTS FULL SIZE.

No. 948. [PYRAMID].......$1 80   No. 923. [QUACK]........$1 80   No. 913. [QUACKING].....$1 80   No. 939. [QUADRATE].....$1 80

FILLED AND ROLLED PLATE VEST CHAINS.

Two, Three, or Four Strands.   All Full Length with Attachment for Charm.

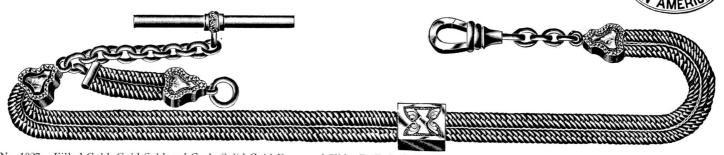

No. 1027.   Filled Gold, Gold Soldered Curb, Solid Gold Engraved Slide, R. F. S. & Co...Each $12 00

No. 1028.   New Three Strand Curb, W. & S. B.........   Each $8 00

No. 1038.   Engraved Gold Slide and Tips, W. & S. B. ★ Each $12 00

Multi-strand vest chains from 1895.

LADIES' VICTORIA CHAINS.

W. & S. B.'s ★ "Old Reliable" Finest Rolled Gold Plate all Polished Chains and Charms.

No. 854.   Each..$3 00
Woven Wire Chain,
Ornamented Charm.

No. 855.   Each..$3 25
Woven Wire Chain.

No. 856.   Each..$3 25
Polished Fox Tail,
Chased Charm.

No. 857.   Each..$3 50
Woven Wire,
Ornamented Charm.

No. 858.   Each..$3 25
Balloon Links,
Ornamented Charm.

No. 859.   Each..$4 00
Engraved Gold
Sides Charm.

Ladies' Victoria chains from 1895.

Opposite: Vest chains made of white
metal, gold plate and gilt.

SOLID WHITE METAL VEST CHAINS.

Best English Make.   White all through.

No. 1221.   Plain Curb..Per Doz. $1 60
No. 1222.   "   "   with Crystal Charm...........................   "   2 75

No. 1223.   With Tips..Per Doz. $3 50
No. 1224.   Without Tips..   "   2 00
No. 1225.   "   "   with Crystal Charm...........................   "   3 25

No. 1226.   With Tips..Per Doz. $4 00
No. 1227.   Without Tips..   "   2 50
No. 1228.   "   "   with Crystal Charm...........................   "   3 75

No. 1229.   With Tips..Per Doz. $4 50
No. 1230.   Without Tips..   "   3 00

No. 1231.   Extra Heavy Curb....................................Per Doz. $4 50

No. 1232.   Rope Pattern, with Charm Attachment.................Per Doz. $3 75

No. 1233.   Two Strand Curb......................................Per Doz. $5 00

Lot No. 1234.   Per Lot, $3 50   { Consists of 12 assorted patterns, Long Links, Trace Links and Fancy Links, Solid White Metal Gents' Vest Chains, with Charm Attachment, Soldered Links, extra quality and finish, on velvet card.

Lot No. 1235.   Per Lot, $4 00   { Consists of 12 assorted patterns, Long Links, Trace Links and Fancy Links, Solid White Metal Vest Chains, with Charm Attachment, small, neat sizes, for boys, on velvet card.

SILVER PLATED ON STEEL VEST CHAINS.

No. 1236. $3 00   { Contains 1 dozen assorted patterns, Gents' Vest Chains, Silver Plated on Steel.
See page 467 for Steel Chains.

ELECTRO GOLD PLATE VEST CHAINS.

No. 1237.   Fancy Long Links.....................................Per Doz. $4 50

No. 1238.   Fancy Long Links.....................................Per Doz. $4 50

No. 1239.   California Links, with Nugget Charm..................Per Doz. $4 50

No. 1240.   Fancy Long Links.....................................Per Doz. $4 50

Lot No. 1241. Per Lot, $4 00   { Contains 1 dozen assorted patterns of above Chains. This number only in full dozens.

No. 1242.   Trace Link, with Coin Shape Charm.   Sold only in full dozens...........Per Doz. $1 25

FIRE GILT VEST CHAINS.

Full Length, Attachments for Charms

No.
1243.   Assorted Long Links, Doz. $11 00
1244.   Full dozen, 12 kinds, for.. 10 00

No. 1245.
Doz..........$9 00
Plain Links.

No. 1246.
Doz..........$9 00
Assorted Fancy Links.

Watches

Pocket watches seemed to rank first on the list of important jewelry. Catalogs always pictured the watches before anything else. The *BHA (Busiest House in America) Illustrated Catalogue* for 1895 pictured, described and priced hundreds of watch cases and movements. The watch cases were sold separately in the catalog. This enabled the buyer to pick out the case and choose the movement he desired. Prices ranged from $3.00 for a gold-electroplated case to $125.40 for a solid gold hunting case. This was an extravagant sum to pay at that time. The watch cases were spread over 50 pages of the catalog. These wonderful, extremely ornamental watches were sold to both men and women.

Jewelry styles went through many changes in the decades preceding the twentieth century. By the end of the period, the amount of jewelry worn had dwindled. Earrings and necklaces became smaller and more delicate; bracelets became thinner. The style was changing from the bold and massive look to a more refined and simple look. Portrait pins, using photographs, became popular by the end of the nineteenth century. Though hair jewelry was used initially to commemorate the dead, the mood gradually changed wherein portrait pins honored the living. Fashionable people were tired of mourning; a time for a change was drawing near.

No. 4633. 16 Size, Hunting...[BANTAIN] $9 50
No. 4634. 16 Size, Open Face. [BANTER] 8 60
Albata Caps and Gold Joints.

No. 4226. 18 Size, Hunting [APPOSITELY] $15 50
No. 4227. 18 Size, Open Face [APPRAISE] 14 00

Men's 10K and 14K gold filled watch cases from 1895.

No. 4453. 6 Size, Hunting,
with Rose Diamond......$21 00
[ATROCIOUS.]
No. 4454. 6 Size, Hunting,
with Diamond Brilliant... 25 00
[ATROCITY.]

No. 4431. 6 Size, Hunting..$29 00
[ASUNDER.]

No. 4432. 6 Size, Hunting..$14 00
[ASYLUM.]

Ladies' gold filled watch cases from 1895.

Gay Nineties

In the last decade of the nineteenth century, more commonly called the "Gay Nineties," the mood did change. The strict discipline imposed in England by Queen Victoria was coming to an end. Women were becoming liberated; they took part in outdoor activities such as sailing, cycling and golf. Fashion and accessories changed to fit their needs. Victorian England was changing but still not as fast as the rest of the world. France always seemed to be a leader in European fashion. By the end of the century, many master craftsmen were centered in Paris. Two completely different styles of jewelry were simultaneously developing: early twentieth century opulence and Art Nouveau.

Six portrait pins in brass frames, circa 1895-1910. $50-75 each.

Chatelaine purse made of silver gilt and set with turquoise stones cut *en cabochon,* circa 1885. $200-250.

Coin holder in the shape of a locket, embossed design, made of gilded brass, circa 1890-1895. $90-120.

No. 288. Each, $12 00
Fine Dark Topaz,
Extra Heavy.

No. 289. Each, $11 00
Fine Garnet,
Extra Heavy.

No. 294. Each, $10 50
Fine Garnet,
Extra Heavy.

No. 295. Each, $10 00
Fine Garnet,
Extra Heavy.

No. 300. Each, $15 00
Extra Heavy.

No. 301. Each, $11 00

No. 306. Each, $5 25
Carbuncle Moss Agate,
Heavy.

No. 307. Each, $5 00
Encrusted Amethyst.

No. 312. Each, $12 50
Opal, Ruby Eyes.

No. 313. Each, $11 00
Ruby Doublets.

Finger rings for men and women pictured in the BHA Illustrated Catalog of 1895.

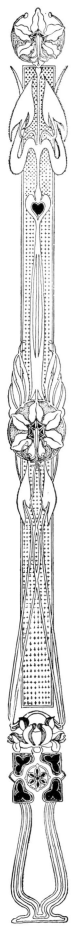

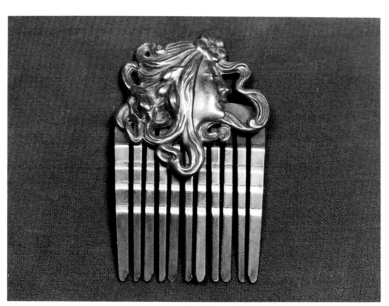

Hair comb made of brass with repoussé design of a woman with flowing hair, circa 1900-05. $90-120.

Opposite:
Brooch made of gilded brass with bezel-set imitation opal, circa 1905-1910. $45-60.

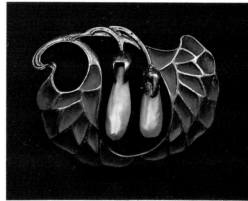

Brooch of silver gilt, *pliqué a jour* enamel and natural pearls, made by Ernst Gideon Bek, hallmark - a butterfly, circa 1895. *Her Own Place.* $850.

Locket made of gilded brass with raised ornamentation of a woman with flowing hair accented with brilliants, circa 1905. $85-120.

Extremely large brass pendant in the shape of a leaf with a stylized woman holding an extended lily representing purity and innocence, circa 1900. $250-300.

Chapter Two
Art Nouveau

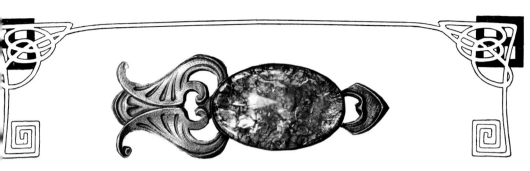

As the end of the nineteenth century drew near, a sinuous style of design swept through Europe. The term *Art Nouveau*, which means "new art," possessed an exotic and sometimes erotic influence resulting in shapes representing free-flowing hair, sensuous nude bodies, flowers and insects in asymmetrical form. Colors often were attained by enameling rather than through a mixture of assorted gemstones. The new craftsman preferred the use of glass and semiprecious stones. It was a new movement involving a refusal to conform to the industrialized society that had evolved. Designers and craftsmen were opposed to mass production and the redundant use of previous styles. There became a movement for man against machine and an apparent craft revival.

Materials

The Art Nouveau style was seen in all forms of decorative arts. Glassware, furniture, posters and jewelry were made in this new and sometimes bizarre style. Metals such as bronze, copper, brass and aluminum were used in addition to gold and silver. Horn, ivory, tortoiseshell, obsidian and glass became popular at this time. Semiprecious stones such as lapis, malachite, azurite and chrysoprase were favored by artisans and made into elaborate buckles, brooches, necklaces and hair ornaments. When gemstones were employed, they were cut *en cabochon* rather than faceted. The main reason for using gemstones was decorative. The beauty of the stone was far more important than its actual value. To create an object of beauty by choosing materials for their natural qualities rather than their intrinsic value was what the craftsman of the Art Nouveau movement was striving for.

Motifs

As in previous periods, the craftsman used motifs from nature, but at times they were greatly exaggerated. Irises, serpents, bats, butterflies, lilies and dragonflies were common themes. They were incorporated artistically in a mode of fantasy rather than reality. As the movement progressed, some of the pieces became too elaborate to wear. The jewelry was unlike anything ever seen before. Some people rejected it while others adored it.

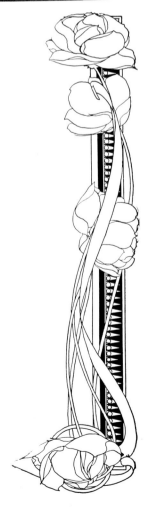

Bracelet and two lace pins made of brass and molded glass stones, circa 1905-1910. $35-75 each.

Art Nouveau pendant made of brass with opaque red celluloid center and smaller imitation ruby accents, circa 1900-1905. The chain on this pendant is Victorian. $65-85.

Morris

The roots of the Art Nouveau movement started in England around the mid-nineteenth century. There, influenced by William Morris, was initiated the Arts and Crafts movement, incorporating what would be Art Nouveau ideals. Morris was opposed to mass production and the Industrial Revolution, feeling no artist should be a slave to machinery. He believed in hand work and wanted artists to express themselves in that manner. Because of this, products created by Morris were very expensive, as hand work usually is. Unfortunately, the average worker could not afford his creations.

Mackmurdo and Ashbee

Other innovators in the movement were English designers Arthur Heygate Mackmurdo and Charles Robert Ashbee. In 1882, Mackmurdo founded the Century Guild. Ashbee started the Guild and School of Handicraft in London in 1888. Ashbee based his style of jewelry design on the common forms of nature. Flowers, especially the rose and the carnation, were two of his favorites. He cleverly employed silver and gold along with amethysts, opals, turquoise and blister pearls in designs executed by the Guild. The peacock was another favorite in Ashbee's designs. The Guild members believed in hand work and were opposed to machine-made art. This arts and crafts revival, with leaders like Morris, Mackmurdo and Ashbee, led to the birth of Art Nouveau.

Glasgow Four

In Scotland, Charles Rennie Mackintosh and his wife Margaret MacDonald along with Herbert and Frances McNair, made up a group called the "Glasgow Four." Their work was very different from the rest of the artisans in the new British artistic jewelry movement. At times, it was frowned upon for being too different or even "spooky," but traces of another style could be seen in their work. The Glasgow School of Art later influenced Austrian, German and Belgian jewelry designers. Josef Hoffman, who founded the *Wiener Werkstatte* (Vienna Workshops) in 1903 was especially influenced by the Glasgow Four. British Art Nouveau reached its most advanced expression in Glasgow, Scotland.

Art Nouveau was not one particular style but a fusion of many styles incorporated into elaborate designs made mostly by hand. Other influences in the movement were Japanese art and culture, with elements of Baroque, Gothic, Renaissance and Celtic art.

France

Lalique

Although a tremendous amount of creativity emerged from England during this movement, the French also excelled in this new art style. Paris had become a breeding ground for creative genius and many master craftsmen emerged from Paris around the turn of the century. Rene' Lalique qualifies as a true master of his craft. After working as an apprentice for some well-known Parisian jewelers, Lalique went to England where he became interested in the "new art" movement. In 1881 he returned to Paris, resuming his work with notable firms such as Cartier and Boucheron. Ten years later, with a commission to make jewelry for Sarah Bernhardt, the leading actress of the theatre, Lalique was finally recognized for the genius he was. He became an expert in the art of stained glass. The *plique á jour* method of enameling became the basis of some of his most exquisite pieces of jewelry.

At the 1900 World's Fair in Paris, admiration for Lalique had grown so that when his jewelry was shown there, Queen Victoria was among those who purchased some of his work. Lalique's creativity and imagination influenced many other designers and craftsmen, but no one really mastered his techniques. He was concerned with the artistic merit of the materials he used rather than their monetary value. As with other notable French jewelers of this period, Lalique viewed precious stones as secondary. He incorporated gold, ivory, chrysoprase, amber, horn, silver and various enameling techniques into his designs which became fantastical interpretations of flora and fauna. Lalique is also noted for incorporating the female nude in his jewelry designs.

Fouquet

Goldsmith George Fouquet should also be acknowledged for his contributions to the Art Nouveau style. Along with leading poster designer of the period Alphonse Mucha, Fouquet made the very famous and very expensive snake bracelet and attached ring for Sarah Bernhardt. Mucha and Fouquet worked well together creating wonderful forms of Art Nouveau jewelry.

Germany

Jugendstil was the name given to the Art Nouveau style in Germany. Although similar to what was seen in England and France, the German designers favored the abstract or geometric styles more than the naturalistic. Eventually, the geometric would win out and Pforzheim, Germany would become a leader in the manufacture of geometric jewelry during the Art Deco period.

Italy

In Italy, *Stile Liberty*, named after Liberty and Company in London, was the term applied to the Art Nouveau style there. Liberty

Earrings made of oxidized brass set with imitation chrysoprase and moonstones, circa 1900-1905. $60-80.

Necklace in sterling silver with bezel-set chrysoprase stone cut *en cabochon* and chrysoprase drop, circa 1900. $125-175.

acquired vast amounts of Japanese goods that had not been sold during the 1862 London Exhibition. He helped promote an interest in Japanese art and culture. This influenced craftsmen and designers to incorporate Oriental motifs into their designs.

Denmark

In Denmark, Georg Jensen symbolized Art Nouveau with the use of cabochon-cut stones set in silver. The Danish designs were heavier but more streamlined than those seen in other countries. Jensen also used tortoiseshell and silver when making combs, along with amber, one of his favorite materials. Jensen stood out among his contemporaries as having a style all his own.

Austria

In Austria, jewelry manufacturing was centered in Vienna. *Sezession* (Secession) was the term applied to the Art Nouveau style there. Viennese jewelers were remarkable in their ability to create unusual designs in ornamental settings. Some of them may be classified as "Baroque," or extremely ornate. Even though the jewelry was ornamental, some of it had geometric aspects as well. Well-balanced curved and straight lines resulted in jewelry of exceptional beauty. As with the French, the Austrians viewed precious stones as secondary. They cleverly utilized colored enamel, semiprecious stones and cut glass in their designs.

Bohemia

In Bohemia, Art Nouveau was known as *Recession* while Spain used the term *Juventud*. Every country in Europe seemed to have a different name for the style that incorporated common aesthetic principles.

Handy pins offered from *McCall's* in 1912.

Buckle made of gilded brass with flower ornamentation, circa 1905. $45-75.

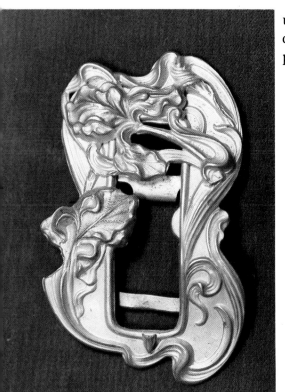

Sash pin made of brass with silver gilt set with blue glass stone, circa 1905. $90-110.

Belgium

Belgian Art Nouveau designers used the naturalistic motifs more than the Germans and the Austrians. They preferred colored gemstones over excessive enameling. Philippe Wolfers was a noted Belgian designer who had already been established as a crown jeweler to the Belgian court. Wolfers easily adapted his style to the "new art" movement since he was very much interested in nature. Enameled pheasants were wrapped around sapphires; black enameled serpents encircled gold nudes. These were common themes used in his designs but he did not limit himself to these. The precious stones that he employed were symbolic to his designs. He wanted his jewelry to speak for itself; in essence, to convey a message. Wolfers was a true artist and later became interested in sculpture.

America

Tiffany

One of the greatest American decorators of the twentieth century was Louis Comfort Tiffany. Tiffany was the son of New York store owner Charles Lewis Tiffany who specialized in unusual *objets d'art*. He started his career as an oil painter but is remembered more for his stained glass lamps and opalescent art glass. Tiffany was associated with gallery owner Samuel Bing of Paris. Bing, like Liberty of London, was a dealer in Japanese art. Tiffany purchased many fine pieces of Japanese art from Bing, with whom he developed a good relationship and shared common interests and ideas. Unlike William Morris, Tiffany and Bing had good feelings for the new machine age. They felt that machines could be useful in producing many beautiful creations in quantity. They both believed in a new type of art. It was in Paris that Art Nouveau acquired its name. On December 26, 1895.

Amethyst brooch offered as a premium for subscribing to *McCall's* Magazine in 1910.

Brooch made of sterling silver, circa 1989. This is a reproduction of an authentic Art Nouveau style brooch made at the turn of the century. $30-50.

Enameled brass brooch, circa 1905. $50-75.

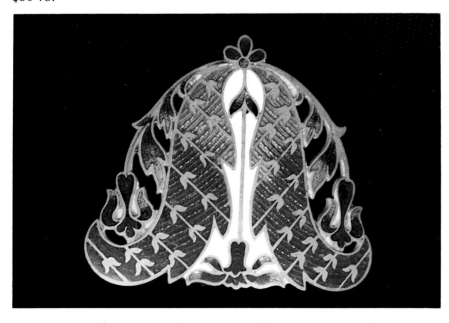

Samuel Bing's gallery *La Maison de l'Art Nouveau* staged a public exhibition of works by Tiffany, Mackintosh, Henri de Toulouse-Lautrec, Aubrey Beardsley and others. Paris had become the stage for this new extravagant movement.

Although L.C. Tiffany today is noted for his fabulous stained glass, he also produced picture frames, trinket boxes, cigarette cases, lighters, clocks and perfume bottles. The jewelry made by Tiffany included hair ornaments, necklaces, buckles, bracelets, cuff links, watch chains and rings. He utilized precious and semiprecious stones along with gold and exquisite enamel work. Tiffany may be credited with bringing the Art Nouveau style to America.

Lavaliere made of brass and imitation pearl. This particular style of Art Nouveau jewelry is being reproduced today. $65-85.

Collar pin offered as a premium for subscribing to *To-Day's Magazine* in 1911.

Premium 335
HANDSOME COLLAR PIN
For only Two Subscriptions
This beautiful Gold Plated Brooch or Collar Pin is in the latest green gold color, and is set with a beautiful imitation 24 facet Topaz stone. The brooch is exactly the size of the above illustration, which however, fails to do justice to this really beautiful piece of jewelry. This handsome pin is well made in every respect and will wear for years. We will send it prepaid to any address for securing only two yearly subscriptions.

Sash pin in rolled gold plate set with pink glass stones, marked C&R, circa 1905-1910. $135-150.

Brooch in gilded brass with topaz-colored glass stone and snake ornamentation, circa 1900-1905. $60-75.

Brooch made of brass and green glass stones, circa 1910. This particular piece is being reproduced today. $40-60.

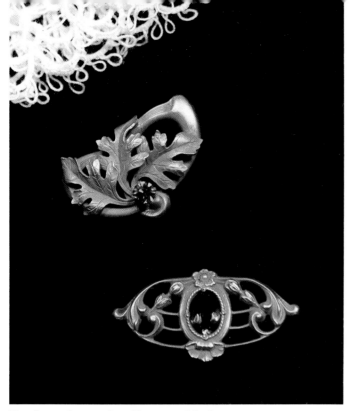

Necklace in silver gilt and square and rectangular-cut blue glass stones, circa 1910-1915. $70-85.

Two lace pins made of brass and imitation stones, circa 1905-1910. $45. each.

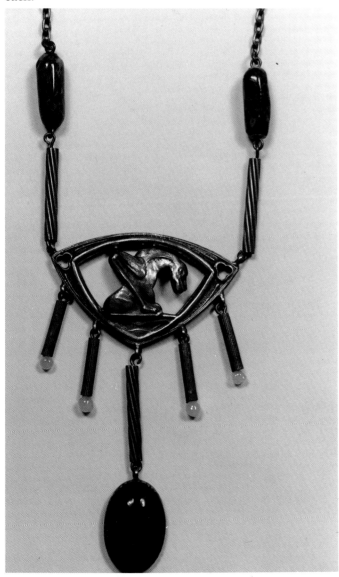

Bar pin of brass in openwork design with imitation pearl and sapphire accents, circa 1905-1910. $50-65.

Necklace in silver gilt with stylized animal motif and simulated lapis stones, circa 1900-1910. $65-85.

Edwardian fashion for 1905.

Chapter Three

Edwardian

The period of opulence was rather short-lived, lasting about a decade from 1901 until 1910. The style itself dates from the Gay Nineties of the previous century and traces of it could be found until the onset of World War I.

The opulent era in England referred to as the Edwardian era is named after Queen Victoria's eldest son, Edward. By 1897, the year of Queen Victoria's Diamond Jubilee, the restrained Victorian epoch had virtually come to an end. King Edward VII was a rather conservative but debonair man. Being a more relaxed monarch, Edward imposed less discipline than his predecessor, Queen Victoria. Edward's Queen, Alexandra, daughter of the King of Denmark, was a beautiful woman and she influenced fashion for years before she was actually crowned. Both Edward and Alexandra created an atmosphere of glitter and sparkle which fascinated the public. The Edwardian era ushered in a dazzling array of beautiful fashions and accessories.

Dog-collar necklaces

Dog-collar necklaces were first seen in France around 1865. By 1880, the style had caught on in England. Traditionally, dog collars consisted of wide bands of velvet or black moire garnished with diamonds and pearls for the rich and paste stones and glass beads for the less affluent. Eventually, the fabric was excluded altogether and the dog collar consisted solely of gemstones in stylized patterns. Occasionally, pearl dog collars were made of up to twenty strands of pearls. Dog collars were fashionable during the last two decades of the nineteenth century and remained popular until around 1914. Queen Alexandra wore them frequently for evening wear. *Designer* magazine for January 1905 makes a reference to this particular jewel:

> The dog collar made of real or French jewels is high in popular favor. In many instances it takes the place of a collar, and is worn becomingly in that capacity. Rather deep collars, set with huge amethysts, are all the rage and may be owned at reasonable cost. Many of the imitation jewels are irresistible, and since this is a year of gleam, too much stress cannot be placed upon their value as a charming dress acquisition.

Photo Copyright by Marceau

MRS. GEORGE GOULD

Edwardian diamond dog collar, pearls and jeweled tiara worn by Mrs. George Gould in 1911.

Chatelaine made of gilded silver with all five implements hallmarked 1875-1895. *Her Own Place.* $650-800.

Chatelaine made of gilded brass with repoussé work, set with simulated rubies, circa 1890-1895. $250-300.

Chatelaines

Alexandra also popularized the use of chatelaines which had gone out of style in the 1860s when she began using them herself in the 1890s.

Chatelaine, used for carrying coins, made of brass and set with imitation emeralds, circa 1890-1895. $250-300.

Silver-plated chatelaine, English, circa 1875. *Her Own Place.* $195.

Lavalieres

Around 1900, the lavaliere came into vogue. This type of necklace usually consists of a pendant which is suspended from a long chain. Some lavalieres consist of two pendants attached to a fine chain with a center sliding motif; and still others are fashioned in the lariat style, where two pendants, overlapped, hang in different lengths.

Lavaliere made of 10K gold with delicate pierced and engraved work, set with genuine amethyst and natural pearls, circa 1905-1910. $225-275.

Lavaliere made of sterling silver, accented with brilliants and enamel work, circa 1910. $100-125.

Lavaliere made of aluminum and set with brilliants, circa 1905-1910. $125-150.

Lavaliere in gilt and lapis, circa 1910-1915. $75-100.

Two citrine-colored cut glass lavaliers made in the lariat style, circa 1910-1920. $50-75 each.

Lavaliere of 10K yellow gold set with moonstone, amethyst and pearl drop, circa 1905-1910. $150-175.

38155
11.50

38154
27.50

38156 50.00

38157
4.50

38158
5.50

SOLID WHITE GOLD PENDANTS AND LAVALLIERES

We illustrate here a special selection of the very newest designs in Solid White Gold Pendants and LaVallieres. Those that are Diamond mounted are set with perfectly cut blue-white stones of fine brilliancy and a 15 inch Solid White Gold chain is included with each. Illustrations show exact sizes.

38154U Platinum front Pendant in a finely pierced and engraved design backed with 14K Solid White Gold, mounted with a perfectly cut blue-white Diamond and a synthetic blue Sapphire. Price including 30 inch black silk neck cord **$27.50**

38155U 14K Solid White Gold Pendant with Diamond mounted in White Gold ornamentations on Black Onyx **$11.50**

38156U 18K Solid White Gold Pendant mounted with a perfectly cut blue-white Diamond and two Genuine Pearls and three square cut blue Sapphires. . . . **$50.00**

38157U Solid White Gold finely pierced Pendant mounted with a synthetic **$4.50** blue Sapphire . . . .

38158U Solid White Gold LaValliere with large center stone surrounded with Seed Pearls and ornamented with Indestructible Pearls. This LaValliere can be furnished with

Circa 1927.

Edwardian brooch of gilded brass and set with brilliants, circa 1905. $150-200.

Earrings made of sterling silver set with brilliants in laurel leaf pattern and imitation pearl drop, circa 1905. $70-95.

Cartier-style brooch made of sterling silver with platinol plate and set with brilliants, circa 1905-1910. $350-400.

House of Cartier

One particular family of outstanding court jewelers that must be mentioned when discussing this period is the Cartier family. Alfred Cartier was born in 1841. In 1874, he took over the family business that his father, Louis-Francois Cartier had established in Paris in 1847. Alfred had three sons: Louis, Pierre and Jacques. The three Cartier brothers eventually built up a very successful business with branches in Paris, London and New York. They were outstanding jewelers and their customers were among the wealthiest people in the world.

Around 1904, The House of Cartier was appointed official jeweler to the court of King Edward VII and Queen Alexandra. Both the King and Queen commissioned many exquisite pieces of jewelry from Cartier. The London branch, opened in 1903, was supervised by Jacques Cartier. Pierre Cartier took control of the branch in New York which opened in 1909. Louis Cartier in Paris was influenced by traditional eighteenth century French court jewelry. His adaptation of the Louis XVI style consisted of bow-knots, tassels, flowers, openwork lace patterns, garland and laurel wreath designs. He was also inspired by Oriental elegance which would become the basis of some of the firm's most exquisite Art Deco designs. The large courtly jewels made by Cartier consisted of stomachers (bodice ornaments), aigrettes, bandeaux, tiaras, *resille'* necklaces (net-like style) and corsage ornaments. They were made in the traditional "garland style." This type of jewelry was commissioned by royalty, nobility and wealthy aristocrats.

Cartier's style exemplifies the elegant and feminine jewelry of this period. Jewelry made by Cartier during the reign of King Edward VII in the first decade of the twentieth century was undoubtedly the epitome of the style. Although Cartier's jewelry is not within the scope of this book, as with other fine jewelers and goldsmiths, Cartier served as an inspiration to craftsmen and jewelers who catered to the less affluent. The style was often imitated, but to a lesser degree of quality. Therefore, traces of Cartier's style is evidenced in some of the jewelry made available to the general public.

Flower basket brooch made of oxidized silver and celluloid flowers, three dimensional, circa 1905-1910. $95-135.

Necklace in sterling silver set with brilliants and square-cut blue glass stones, circa 1905-1910. $100-135.

House of Fabergé

A discussion of early twentieth century jewelry would be incomplete without mentioning the great Peter Carl Fabergé. Little is known about the family of Fabergé before 1842. Carl Fabergé was born in St. Petersburg, Russia in 1846. The family, French Huguenots from Northern France, escaped that country and eventually settled in Russia. Unlike his father, Gustav, who set up a jewelry business in 1842, Carl Fabergé concentrated mainly on *objets d'art*. Small boxes, clocks, icons, fans, animals and flowers were expertly carved from gemstones. He mastered the *guilloche'* (engine-turned) method of enameling and was an expert goldsmith.

Fabergés career was enhanced in 1900 during the Paris World's Fair. It was the first time his Imperial Easter eggs were displayed in a public setting. These unique treasures were commissioned during the reigns of Tsar Alexander III and Tsar Nicholas II of Russia. The tsars presented them to the tsarinas during Easter times. Possibly 57 Imperial Easter eggs were made between 1884 and 1917. Faberges' style was exceptional and his high quality of workmanship set the standard for jewelers who were about to emerge into the twentieth century.

36907U
The Floating Opal Pendant. This pendant consists of a beautiful crystal in which many small opals are floating. This unique design greatly increases their beauty and brilliancy. The mounting is 14K solid gold. A rare and original creation. Black silk neck cord included . . . **$17.50**

Circa 1927.

In England each December 1, Queen Alexandra celebrated her birthday. Every year during Edward's reign, a lavish affair was planned for this day in the Queen's honor. Edward, along with members of the court and close friends would present Alexandra with an *objet d'art* made by Fabergé so this day was looked upon with anticipation. Queen Alexandra's Fabergé collection was said to have been one of the largest in the world. Although it consisted of hundreds of *objets d'art*, it did not include one piece of jewelry. The custom in England at that time was to give the Queen gifts of an impersonal nature. Ornaments designed for adorning the body were not considered appropriate. The purchase of such objects was something the Queen took pleasure in doing herself.

Clothing

Everyone loved to dress up in lavish evening wear. In Europe, the theater was the place to go for an evening of great entertainment. In America, musical comedy or "Vaudeville" was a favorite. The stars of the stage on both sides of the Atlantic influenced fashion tremendously; later the movie screen would have an even greater impact. Charles Dana Gibson, the American cartoonist, depicted the ideal woman a few years earlier with his drawings of the "Gibson Girl." Millions of women wanted to emulate the look of the high coiffure, plunging neckline and the corseted waistline seen in his work. Staunch attitudes displayed by the women of the previous century were vanishing. A "New Woman" was emerging with a flair for life and a new way to live it.

Women of the opulent era wore mannish, tailored suits as well as silk waists, high-necked blouses and sumptuous tea and evening gowns. Jet was still in fashion and evening wear was garnished with jet beads alone or combined with steel, crystal, silver and gold. Couturiers, such as Gaston and Jean-Philippe Worth (sons of the famous fashion designer Charles Frederick Worth), worked side-by-side with jewelers like Cartier producing exquisite garments made of silk and satin; works of art completely encrusted with jewels. The affluent society that had surfaced in Europe and America had a desire to flaunt their material possessions. As a result, lavish garments and elaborate jewels were produced. Smaller firms, catering to the masses, copied and adapted original designs making them affordable to the majority of the population. Undergarments of this period, such as camisoles, petticoats and corsets were also lavishly made. This was the era of the hourglass figure, and corsets made hourglass curves possible. Hats had become extremely large, necessitating use of the hatpin, which in this era reached its peak. Feather boas, fringed shawls, large fur muffs, fans and parasols came into vogue. This was a time when women genuinely wanted to emphasize their femininity and designers catered to that desire. Smaller jewels were fashionable largely because fabrics were so delicate. The exceptions were the courtly jewels mentioned earlier.

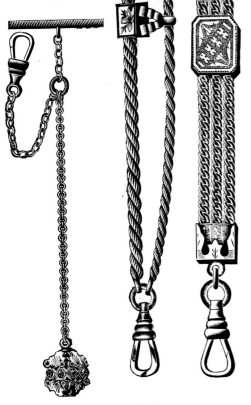

Any single photograph of one or more persons accurately reproduced on inside cap of case or dial of watch $3 50

Photographs being reproduced on pocket watches was a late Victorian and Edwardian fancy. This ad taken from the BHA Illustrated Catalog of 1895.

Stores

Department stores that opened in the nineteenth century grew in number as well as in stature and reached their peak in this era. By the turn of the century, there were close to 1000 department stores in America. Catalogs devoted solely to fashion and accessories came from all over America and Europe. Women could purchase Paris fashion in America and Oriental fashion in England. The Sears, Roebuck and Montgomery Ward catalogs grew from a few pages in the late nineteenth century to a few hundred pages in the first decade of the twentieth century. Fashion was becoming such big business that instead of clothing being featured at the middle or the back of the catalog, it was now featured at the beginning. Styles were endless in variety and the prices, well.... Looking through these catalogs today, one wishes the "Time Machine" was a real invention!

Chains

As in the late nineteenth century, chains were made for every reason. Muff chains, lorgnette chains, fob chains, guard chains, vest chains and watch chains were mass-produced. The "Victoria" and "Albert" chains of the previous century were still being sold. Even coin purses, vanity cases and calling card cases were attached to long chains. Special chains were sold for women's fans. Some chains during this era measured up to 50 inches in length. The Sears and Roebuck Catalog for 1909 displays over 100 styles of vest chains available to men. Prices ranged from $.09 for a gold-plated chain to $6.62 for a gold-filled chain. Sterling silver, gunmetal and other base metals were also used in the manufacture of chains during this period.

Watches

The gentleman was also able to choose from beautifully ornate pocket watches in gold and silver. Animal and railway watch cases were fashionable and much in demand. The smaller ladies' watch was just as popular and came in many styles and price ranges. Some watches had photographs of loved ones on the cases or on the dials. Even though attitudes were changing, traces of disciplined sentiment was still present in this opulent era.

Cuff links

Cuff links or cuff buttons for men and women were extremely ornate. Usually they were made of solid gold, gold filled or rolled gold plate. They were sometimes set with real or imitation diamonds, sapphires, rubies or emeralds. Most cuff buttons were artistically hand engraved and others displayed raised ornamentation. Combination sets, called "shirt waist sets," consisted of a pair of cuff buttons or cuff links, a collar button and a scarf pin. They were sold to both men and women.

SHIRT WAIST SETS.

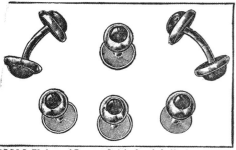

32313 Plain and Roman finish, dumb-bell doz.
style links, polished stone set in as- sets. gro.
sorted colors, 4 buttons to match.. **75 8 50**

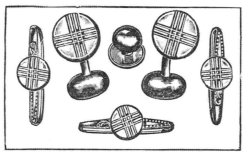

32314 Combination selected polished
pearl grooved pattern and dumb- doz.
bell links, 3 pearl mounted pins sets. gro.
and 1 plain finished collar button.. **80 9 00**

32315 Square and oblong patterns, highly
polished stone set in assorted colors, doz.
3 embossed pins to match and 1 sets. gro.
collar button....................... **85 9 75**

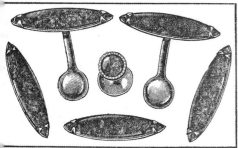

32316 Plain finished, assorted polished stone doz.
set, oval pattern cuff buttons, 3 large pins sets.
and one beaded edge stone set collar button..................................... **95**

32317 3 patterns, combination fancy embossed doz.
dumb-bell link, 3 embossed pins, 1 collar sets.
button, a very desirable assortment....... **95**

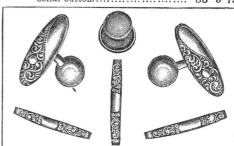

32318 3 patterns, plain and Roman gold finish, doz.
oblong links, embossed front link, 3 pins, sets.
handsome embossed ornaments, and 1
plain collar button...................... **1 10**

32319 New style link buttons, polished stone doz.
settings of assorted colors, 3 plain finished sets.
stone set pins and 1 collar button to match **1 15**

32320 Selected fancy grooved pearl and combi- doz.
nation dumb-bell link, 3 embossed pearl sets.
mounted pins and 1 pearl top collar button to match........................ **1 40**

32321 Roman finish, combination handsome em- doz.
bossed and dumb-bell links, 1 plain collar sets.
button, 3 embossed pins to match, very
desirable patterns................ .... **1 40**

32322 Plain finished, combination dumb-bell doz.
and selected grooved plain pearl links, sets.
very desirable assortment of patterns, 3
embossed pins and 1 plain collar button. **1 40**

32323 6 patterns, plain or Roman finish, heavy doz.
embossed dumb-bell links, 3 richly em- sets.
bossed ornamented pins and 1 collar button to match; good selling line for this
season **1 50**

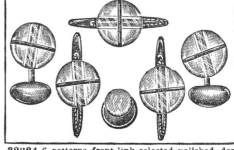

32324 6 patterns, front link selected polished doz.
plain and grooved pattern pearl, gold- sets.
plated wire trimming and dumb-bell links,
3 large pearl mounted pins and 1 pearl top
collar button to match **1 65**

Shirt Waist Sets became popular by
the end of the nineteenth century and
continued to be fashionable throughout the Edwardian period. This jewelry was offered for sale in 1899 from
Lyon Brothers of Chicago.

Chatelettes

Ladies' watch chatelettes, usually taking the *fleur de lis* form were fashionable for hanging a watch or simply worn as a brooch. Some chatelettes came with an attached swivel hook for holding the watch. In the summer when garments were made of lighter fabrics, belt watches were more practical. The *Delineator* magazine for September, 1902 makes this comment about these sporty watches:

> These dainty and refined Belt Watches keep correct time and stand the hard usage incidental to golf and tennis playing, sailing and other outdoor play enjoyed by so many women at this season of the year.

Women of this period were becoming liberated and enjoying every minute of it.

Woman golfer wearing an Edwardian Belt Watch, circa 1902.

Selection of pins and watch chatelettes made of sterling silver, rolled gold plate and gilt in the *fleur de lis* pattern, circa 1900-1910. The large piece in the center is a dress clip made of brass, circa 1930. $25-50 each.

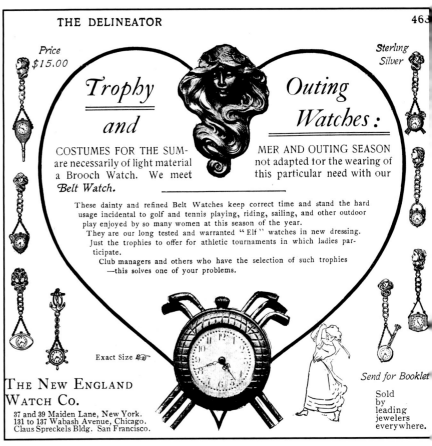

This advertisement for Belt Watches in 1902 clearly displays both the Edwardian and Art Nouveau characteristics of jewelry manufactured around the turn of the century.

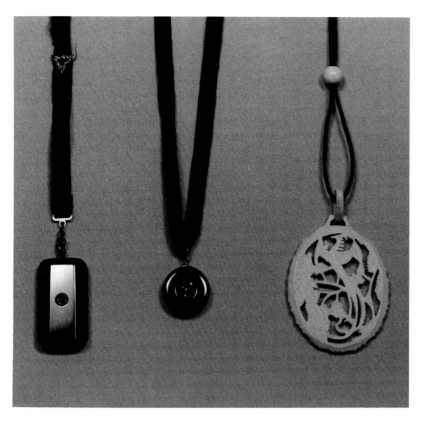

Rectangular *sautoir* of black onyx and iron pyrite on silk grosgrain ribbon with triangular gold filled slide. / Round black onyx and iron pyrite *sautoir.* / Hand-carved Galalith *sautoir* made to look like ivory on black silk cord, circa 1900-1920. $75-150 each.

Lockets

Lockets have always been special; a form of sentimental jewelry that means something even today. A picture or a treasured keepsake was kept within. The lockets of the early twentieth century were smaller than those of the previous century but no less treasured. The most favored lockets were usually heart-shaped, although round, oval and even square lockets were very stylish and mass-produced. They were fashioned from gold, silver or brass; some were heavily ornamented and set with gemstones or brilliants. The styles were endless and many of these nostalgic keepsakes may still be found today.

Two models from Wanamaker's catalog in 1913 wearing an Edwardian bracelet watch and long lavaliere.

Festoon necklaces

Festoon necklaces were still worn during the first decade of the twentieth century but were also made smaller and more delicate than their nineteenth century counterparts. Amber beads had become the rage and most were hand-faceted and graduated, ranging in length from 12 to 18 inches. The 1902 edition of the Sears and Roebuck Catalog makes mention to the remedial qualities of amber:

> It is thought by many, when worn as a necklace, acts as a preventive against colds, sore throats and the contagious diseases' to which children are subject.

Children of the Edwardian period wore amber jewelry for some of the same reasons as the children of the Victorian period wore coral jewelry.

Woman wearing an Edwardian fringed necklace pictured in John Wanamaker's Store and Home Catalog for the summer of 1913.

Gold filled festoon necklace set with aquamarines, circa 1900-1910. $200-250.

Festoon necklace in gold filled with onyx cameo, circa 1900. $125-175.

Two *sautoirs* made of Bohemian glass, brass and gilt, circa 1910. $125-175.

Two genuine amber pendants and a strand of hand-cut cherry amber beads, circa 1920s. Amber pendants, $50-75 each. Amber beads, $300-350.

Pendant necklace made of glass with reverse-carved design suspended from black glass link chain with glass drop. This particular piece is un-marked but it resembles the work of R. Lalique, circa 1910-1915. $275-350.

Flower basket pendant in sterling silver and marcasites, circa 1915. Edwardian/Early Art Deco. $95-135.

Beautiful Edwardian lavaliere made of sterling silver and frosted glass suspended from a silk cord. The flower basket motif on the glass and the *fleur de lis* on the slide are enameled and set with small rubies and emeralds, circa 1905-1910. $350-450.

Two Edwardian *sautoirs* made of brass and Bohemian glass, circa 1905-1910. $90-125 each.

Crystalline diamonds

In the 1908 and 1909 editions of the same catalog, crystalline diamond jewelry is mentioned. It notes that:

> Crystalline Diamonds are worn by actors and actresses and those wanting the most perfect imitations known. We have thousands of professional people, actors and actresses throughout the United States, who buy crystalline diamonds to wear instead of using the genuine article.

Rings, brooches, earrings, pendants and stick pins were set with crystalline diamonds. Most of these imitations were made of rock crystal and set in solid gold, sterling silver or gold-filled mountings. Costume jewelry was beginning to be accepted by people of all walks of life; not only those who could afford nothing better.

Bangle bracelets

Bangle bracelets made their mark in this period. They had been worn in earlier centuries and adapted nicely to the new styles. Most bangle bracelets were thin and elaborately hand engraved or embossed. They were beautifully made of solid gold, gold filled, rolled gold plate or sterling silver. Gold chain curb bracelets were popular in different patterns. They were again adorned with engraving. Flexible spring bracelets and adjustable expansion bracelets were also fashionable in the first decade of the twentieth century.

Five bangle bracelets made of 10K gold and rolled gold plate with hand-engraving and repoussé work. The bracelet in the center is gold filled with *Taille d'epergne* enameling and marked P&H, circa 1890-1910. $150-350.

Gold filled bangle bracelets advertised in the 1908 Sears, Roebuck and Company Catalog No. 117.

Bracelet in openwork design and two lace pins made of brass with a gold wash and set with simulated amethyst stones, circa 1900-1910. Bracelet, $75-100. Two lace pins, $60-85.

Openwork link bracelet in silver gilt set with amethyst-colored glass stones, circa 1910-1915. $65-85.

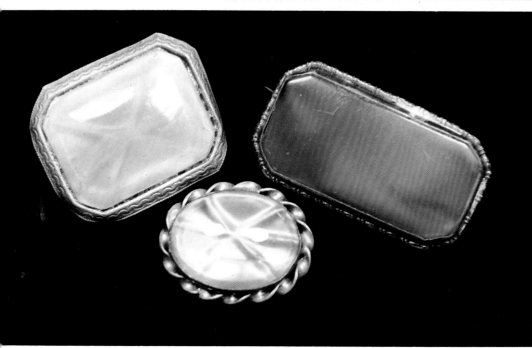

This horse with whip charm made of solid gold retailed for $10 in 1895.

Three brooches set with colored glass stones mounted in silver gilt frames, circa 1910. $25-35 each.

Pins

Sash and belt pins were usually large and ornate; lace and beauty pins were small and delicate. Featured in mail-order catalogs and frequently in magazines, they were offered as free premiums for subscribing to the publication in which they were featured. Lace pins were perfect for the high-necked blouses worn in this period. They added a little "something extra" to the already detailed garment. Lace collars and cuffs to match were "dainty conceits" to be worn over a fancy bodice. Collar pins or "handy pins" as they were sometimes called, were necessary to secure the collar in place at both the front and the back of the garment. These tiny treasures were usually sold in pairs. Scarf and stick pins were also plentiful. Anchors, clovers, crescents, wishbones, flowers and birds were common objects used when designing these delicate pins. Sport-themed jewelry reached an all-time high in this period. Motifs such as riding crops, stirrups, horses and horseshoes were dominant themes.

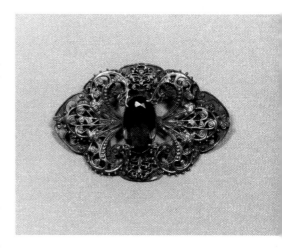

Sash pin made of oxidized brass set with large simulated amethyst, circa 1905. $100-125.

Sash pins made of brass with raised ornamentation and set with simulated rubies, circa 1900-1910. $100-150 each.

Sash pin in gilded brass set with simulated sapphires and genuine marcasites in very ornate setting, circa 1900-1905. $100-125.

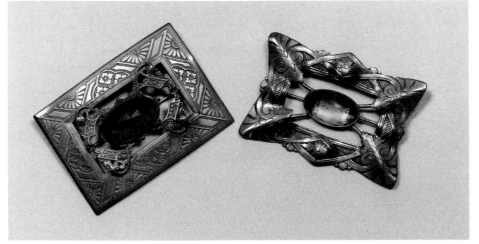

Two sash pins in brass with imitation topaz and amber-colored glass stones, circa 1905-1910. $95-135 each.

Watch chatelette in gold filled with tri-colored gold leaves and inscribed solid gold center, circa 1905. $70-90.

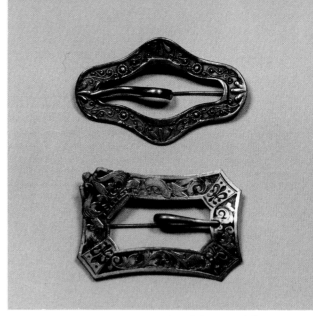

Two sash pins made of brass with simulated hasps, circa 1905-1910. $75-90 each.

Two oval brooches made of brass, circa 1900-1910. $35-45 each.

Bar pin made of rolled gold plate with hand-carved thistle made of topaz-colored glass marked W.Bs, circa 1910. $95-135.

Sterling filigree butterfly with gold wash marked 925, circa 1910. $75-100.

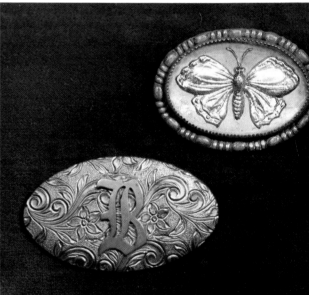

Oval celluloid brooch made to look like tortoiseshell with gold overlay resembling piqué work, marked Made in France, circa 1900-1910. $50-75.

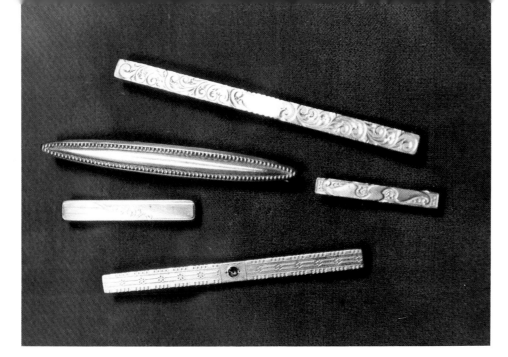

Selection of bar pins and beauty pins made of brass, rolled gold plate and solid gold tops from 1900-1910. $25-75 each.

Large bar pin made of brass and set with simulated topaz, circa 1875. / Bar pin, gold over brass set with garnets and pearl, circa 1885. / Bar pin, gold top, with hand engraving, circa 1890-1900. / Bar pin made of brass with enamel ornamentation, circa 1900-1910. / Bar pin in brass enameled black, circa 1880-1900. / Copper beauty pin set with turquoise stones, circa 1900-1910. / Beauty pin in brass with embossed design, circa 1900-1910. $25-100 each.

Sash pin in brass with green glass stones cut *en cabochon* and simulated hasp, circa 1910. $85-100.

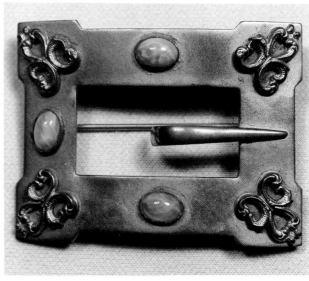

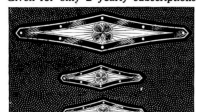

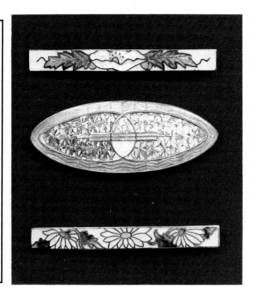

Cloisonné enamel Waist Set offered
as a premium for subscribing to
McCalls Magazine in September of
1902.

A variety of early twentieth century
bar pins, lace and beauty pins of sterling silver, chromium plate and brass
made in the Edwardian and Art
Nouveau styles. $25-75 each.

Two bar pins and oval brooch marked
Genuine Cloisonné Sterling, circa
1905-1910. $75-150.

Hand-painted bar pin set in gilded
brass, circa 1905-1910. $50-75.

Hand-painted bar pin set in brass,
circa 1900-1905. $50-75.

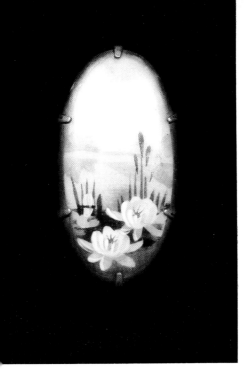

Oval hand-painted porcelain pin in brass frame, circa 1905. $50-75.

Small hand-painted porcelain pin in brass frame, circa 1900. $50-75.

Costume jewelry offered for sale from Chicago's Boston Store in 1910.

Hand-painted porcelain pin in gilded brass frame, circa 1900. $100-150.

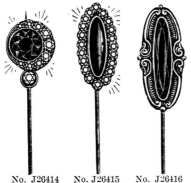
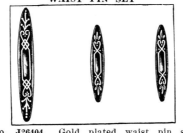

Edwardian ✦ 77

Buckle in gilded brass with cabochon-cut pink glass stones and double hasp, circa 1905-1910. $90-135.

Rings

As with other forms of jewelry, the ring adapted nicely to the dainty and delicate designs of the period. Moonstones, opals and pearls were favorite gems mounted in these delicate settings. Rings for babies and small children were styled almost identically to those for adults.

Buckles and buttons

Cut steel was still very stylish and buckles and buttons made from this material served as garnitures to decorate dresses, coats and hats. Sets of matching buckles and buttons came in various styles and could easily be ordered from catalogs. The 1902 edition of the Sears catalog makes reference to sash buckles:

> They are being worn everywhere by the ladies in all of cosmopolitan cities; they are more than a fad; they have become a necessity. Your costume is not complete without one of our latest ideas in a sash buckle.

Catalogs at this time were really promoting the latest in fashion trends describing these "ornamental conceits" in great detail.

Buckle made of oxidized brass with three bezel-set citrine-colored glass stones, circa 1905-1910. $75-100.

34465U
LINGERIE CLASPS
A fine French cloisonne enamel in a rich, beautiful floral design on sterling silver. A very special value. Per pair...... **75 cts.**

Lingerie clasps, circa 1920.

Shoe buckles made of genuine cut steel. The pair at the bottom are enameled black, circa 1900-1915. $75-100 pair.

Two pairs of cut steel shoe buckles marked France, circa 1905. $75-100 pair.

Edwardian shoe buckles in leather with cut steel trim. $40-65. / Screw-type earrings made of cut steel beads. $30-45. / Small round buckles made of cut steel, circa 1905-1910. $35-50.

Three pairs of shoe buckles: the square and bow-shaped buckles are made of genuine cut steel, $75-100; the round pair are made of imitation cut steel, circa 1900-1910. $25-50.

Edwardian shoe buckles set with brilliants, circa 1905. $75-100.

Silver

In the 1880s in England, silver frequently was used in making jewelry largely due to Queen Victoria's Silver Jubilee in 1887 marking the 50th year of her reign. People wanted to get away from the dull and somber effect jet and other black materials created. For a few years novelty silver jewelry was all the rage. By the 1890s, however, silver had gone out of style somewhat. It enjoyed a revival in popularity about the end of the first decade of the twentieth century.

Platinum

By 1900, the use of platinum in the jewelry industry was reaching an all-time high. Platinum was used primarily for setting diamonds since it greatly enhanced the reflective properties of the diamond. Platinum does not tarnish and it is stronger than silver; this meant that less metal could be used in the settings.

Pendant necklace and bracelet made of silver-plated brass set with opaque red glass stones, circa 1910-1915. $50-75 each.

Assortment of scarf and stick pins made of 14K yellow gold, 10K white gold, sterling silver, brass and gilt from different periods, circa 1880-1920. These pins were worn by both men and women. $45-150 each.

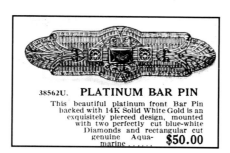

38562U.   **PLATINUM BAR PIN**
This beautiful platinum front Bar Pin backed with 14K Solid White Gold is an exquisitely pierced design, mounted with two perfectly cut blue-white Diamonds and rectangular cut genuine Aqua-marine........ **$50.00**

Platinum bar pin advertised for sale in 1927.

Pendant of sterling silver and camphor glass. $90-145. / Fringed necklace made of brass with clear cut glass drops, circa 1910-1920. $100-150.

Flexible sterling silver bracelet in openwork pattern set with imitation sapphires, circa 1920-1925. $100-150. / Filigree link bracelet with platinol plate and three alternating clear pressed glass stones, circa 1910-1920, $150-200. This is a Transitional piece with Edwardian and Art Deco characteristics.

Edwardian coin purse made of German silver with a 30-inch chain and intermittent crystal beads, circa 1900-1905. $175-225.

Gilded brass flower necklace with genuine carved amber drops, circa 1910-1915. $200-250.

Filigree

Delicate jewelry complemented the fabrics of sumptuous silk dresses and blouses of this period, rich in lace and embroidery. By 1910, filigree jewelry made of platinum, white gold and sterling silver was the height of fashion. Ornamental, openwork lace patterns of the twentieth century were more refined and delicate than the scrolling wire filigree sometimes displayed in jewelry of the nineteenth century.

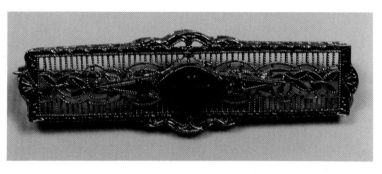

Lavaliere made of silver filigree, camphor glass and brilliant, circa 1910-1915. $100-135.

Filigree bar pin in 10K white gold set with carved green agate and imitation diamonds, circa 1910-1915. $175-225.

38471.
Scarf Pin set with one perfectly cut blue-white Diamond with border of synthetic Blue Sapphires.
$50.00

Circa 1927.

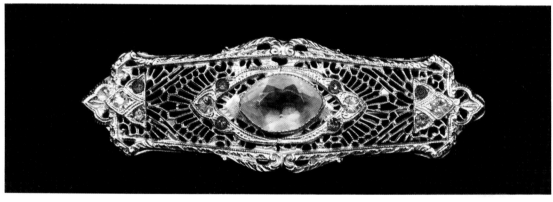

Filigree bar pin in chromium-plated base metal set with a synthetic citrine and rhinestones, circa 1910-1920. $75-100.

Chromium-finished filigree bar pin set with imitation moonstone cut *en cabochon,* circa 1910-1915. $60-90.

Filigree drop earrings in chromium plate with frosted glass stone set with brilliants, late Edwardian / early Art Deco. $75-100.

Sterling silver filigree necklace with three camphor glass (frosted glass) medallions set with brilliants, circa 1910-1920. $125-150.

Hand-made rhinestone bandeau with matching bracelet, circa 1910-1915. $100-150.

Rhinestone bandeau in openwork pattern made of gilded brass, circa 1910. $125-150.

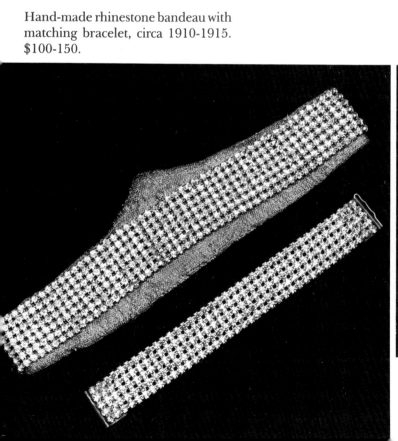

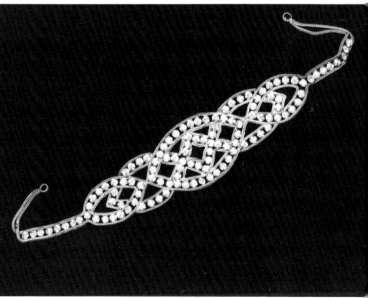

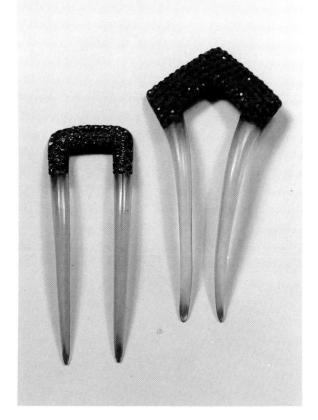

Two celluloid hair pins set with colored glass stones, circa 1905-1910. $40-65 each.

Green celluloid hair comb set with green glass stones. / Hair comb made of celluloid with black overlay and red glass stones. / Gold speckled hair comb, circa 1900-1910. $50-90 each.

Back comb made of gold speckled celluloid set with pink glass stones, circa 1910. $70-90.

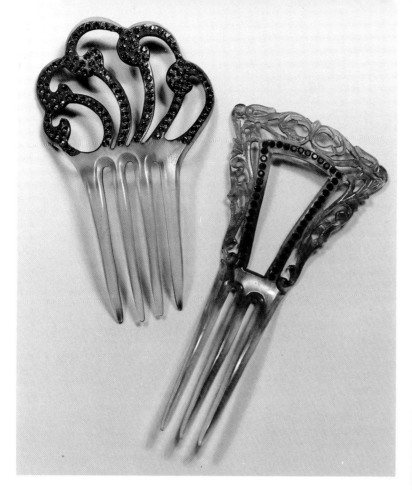

Two celluloid hair combs set with colored glass stones, circa 1905-1910. $60-85 each.

The opulent early twentieth century era was short-lived but it produced a wonderful assortment of jewelry and accessories for both men and women. It was the pinnacle in production of delicate and elegant jewelry, which was nothing like the heavy, massive and sometimes gaudy jewelry of the previous century and completely different from the Art Nouveau style that appealed to segments of the "avant garde" society.

Large decorative hair comb made of celluloid and set with blue glass stones, circa 1905-1910. $100-135.

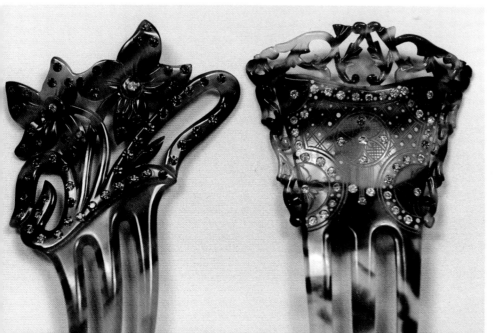

Two turn of the century celluloid hair combs made to look like tortoiseshell. The comb on the left displays Art Nouveau characteristics while the comb on the right displays Edwardian characteristics. $75-100 each.

Necklace and bracelet of brass filigree. Bohemian topaz-colored glass and enamel ornamentation, circa 1910-1918. $175-225 set.

Fringed necklace of brass filigree and green glass beads, marked Made in Czechoslovakia, circa 1918-1922. $90-130.

Three *sautoirs* made of brass and Bohemian glass. / Three brass and glass stick pins, circa 1910-1920. $100-150 each.

Chapter Four

Transitional

Through the ages, jewelry design did not automatically change from one style to another. Changes were gradual, tending to overlap from one period to the next. Long before the Victorian style of the late-nineteenth century era had come to an end, new looks in jewelry were beginning to surface. The ostentatious style of the third quarter of the nineteenth century was dividing itself into the elegant Edwardian "garland" style and the "avant garde" Art Nouveau style by the turn of the century. While these two styles were flourishing, the roots of a modern movement were already beginning to grow. As early as 1903, geometric styles of design were displayed in jewelry made by some designers in the *Wiener Werkstatte*. In other countries, Germany in particular, jewelry began to created with geometric and abstract characteristics very early in the twentieth century. In Czechoslovakia, on the other hand, design was torn between the old and the new. This country played an important role, making important contributions to the production of jewelry.

Bohemia

Many jewelry manufacturers in the late-nineteenth and early twentieth centuries utilized garnets from Mount Kozakov in the eastern section of Bohemia. Imitation jet, colored glass stones and beads also came from Bohemian cottage craftsmen. Bohemia had been known through the years for its excellent glass artisans, ornate designs, and cottage industries.

Czechoslovakia

Bohemia was inhabited by two dominant tribes of people, the Czechs and the Slovaks, who settled in eastern Europe in the fifth century. After World War I ended in 1918, the Czechs and the Slovaks, for their efforts in aiding the Allies, were united as one. They were freed from the dominance of Austria and Hungary. The land upon which they lived was now called Czechoslovakia. Prior to World War I, the jewelry from this area was termed Bohemian; after World War I, this same jewelry was marked *Czecho-slovakia, Czechoslovakia,* or *Made in Czechoslovakia.* This particular European jewelry has a unique style that should not be classified solely as Art Nouveau or Art Deco. It is a mixture of curvilinear as well as rectilinear lines resulting in very ornate settings. This transitional phase which began about 1910-1914 at the end of the opulent and Art Nouveau periods lasted until the peak of Art Deco in the mid-1920s. It resulted in the production of ornamental treasures made of brass and glass. In order to accurately date period jewelry, this style, made prior to the 1925 Paris Exhibition, will be termed Transitional.

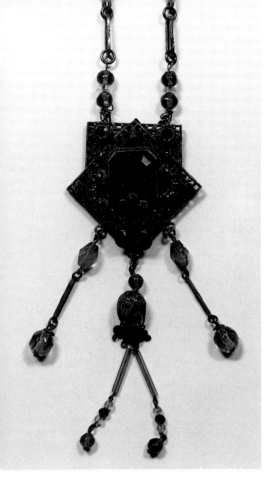

Czechoslovakian jewelry made during the 1930s displayed more of the geometric characteristics that we associate with the Art Deco movement. During this decade, many of the Czechoslovakian glass artisans came to the United States to work. They produced Art Deco style jewelry, perfume bottles and atomizers. They were fond of cut glass in various colors and delicate enamel work.

Czechoslovakian as well as Austrian jewelry is usually marked. After viewing a few pieces, it becomes easy to recognize due to its rather ornamental nature. If you suspect that a certain piece of jewelry was made in Czechoslovakia and it is not marked that way, very possibly it could be a pre-World War I Bohemian piece. This beautiful costume jewelry was extremely fashionable in the early twentieth century and is particularly desirable today.

Ornate *sautoir* made of oxidized brass, blue glass stones and beads on 22-inch chain, marked Made in Austria, circa 1910-1920. $250-325.

Austrian *sautoir* made of oxidized brass with bezel-set topaz-colored glass stones and drops on 22-inch beaded chain, circa 1910-1920. (Art Nouveau/Transitional) $250-325.

Brass locket with red glass stone suspended from 14-inch brass and glass chain, circa 1920. $75-100. / Brass and red glass *sautoir* marked Austria, circa 1915. $150-200. / Pendant necklace in brass and red glass, marked Made in Czechoslovakia, circa 1918-1922. $75-100.

Fringed brooch of topaz-colored pressed glass beads to form a flower and brass chains suspending five pressed glass dangles, circa 1915. $100-125.

Ornate necklace made of brass filigree with imitation amethyst and emerald stones and drops, marked Made in Austria, circa 1910-1920. $100-145.

Two bracelets made of brass and Bohemian glass, circa 1910-1918. $95-145 each.

Cut and pressed glass beads similar to the work of René Lalique, unmarked, circa 1910-1920. *Her Own Place.* $125-175.

Parure consisting of necklace, bracelet and pierced earrings made of gilded brass and simulated turquoise stones, marked Made in Czechoslovakia, circa 1918-1920. $350-400.

Beautiful trio of pressed glass necklaces, resembling the work of Lalique,
circa 1910-1920. $125-175 each.

Bohemian glass and brass necklace
with beaded chain, circa 1910-1918.
$95-130.

Bohemian glass and brass necklace.
$75-100. / Brooch made of enameled
brass and simulated emerald cut *en
cabochon,* circa 1915. $50-65.

Very ornate brass and green glass necklace made in Czechoslovakia, circa 1918-1920. $75-100. / Necklace and matching brooch made of brass and Bohemian glass, circa 1910-1918. $125-150 set.

Necklace and matching bracelet made of brass and Bohemian glass, circa 1910-1915. (Art Nouveau/Transitional). $200-250 set.

Three brass and amethyst-colored glass necklaces marked Czechoslovakia, circa 1918-1925. $95-145 each.

Bracelet made of brass, opaque pink glass stones, and enamel decoration. $75-95. / Necklace made of brass, opaque pink glass and enamel, circa 1910-1920. (Art Nouveau/Transitional). $95-135.

Necklace of oxidized brass filigree links and alternating pink glass stones, marked Czechoslovakia. $90-130. / Brooch of gilded brass filigree and pink glass stones, marked Czechoslovakia. $60-75. / Necklace in silver gilt with pink glass accents, circa 1918-1925. $75-120.

Two Bohemian glass and brass necklace, circa 1910-1918. $125-150 each.

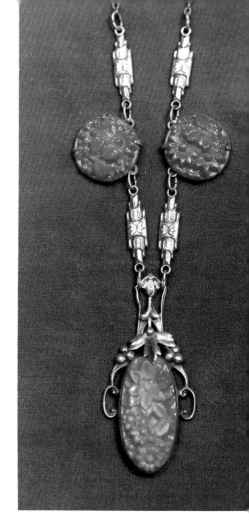

Left to right:
Gilded brass necklace, extremely ornate setting, with topaz-colored glass stones and beads marked Czechoslovakia, circa 1918-1920. $110-140.

Necklace made of brass and opaque red glass stones marked Czechoslovakia, circa 1918-1920. $90-130.

Necklace in sterling silver set with molded glass stones made to look like carved coral, circa 1910-1920. (Art Nouveau/Transitional). $150-175.

Necklace of brass in openwork pattern set with a cobalt blue glass stone cut *en cabochon* and cobalt blue glass drops, circa 1915-1920. $85-125.

Necklace in gilded brass and square-cut blue glass stones marked Czechoslovakia, circa 1918. / Bracelet of gilded brass in openwork pattern encrusted with blue glass stones. $90-140 each.

Bracelet elaborately made of brass and Bohemian glass, circa 1910-1918. $95-145.

Very ornate necklace in gilded brass with blue glass stones and enamel ornamentation, marked Czechoslovakia, circa 1918-1920. $125-175.

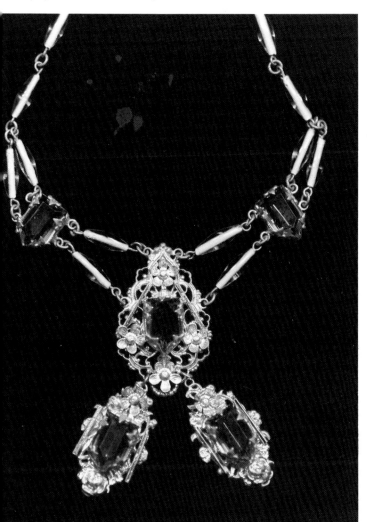

Very ornate brooch made of brass and blue glass stones, marked Czechoslovakia, circa 1920. $75-100.

Brooch made of brass with bezel-set green glass stones, circa 1910-1915. $60-80. / Brass filigree brooch set with green glass stones, marked Czechoslovakia, circa 1918-1920. $45-65.

Choker made of blue glass ovals and round blue rhinestones set in frosted glass collets. $70-90. / Brooch made of gilt and blue glass stones, circa 1910-1920. $65-85.

Ornate brass pendant with large topaz-colored glass stones and enamel ornamentation, circa 1910-1920. (Art Nouveau/Transitional). $125-175.

Two piece brass buckle, openwork setting, with triangular-cut blue glass stones, circa 1915-1920. $70-90.

Pendant necklace made of brass and Bohemian glass, circa 1910-1915. $80-120.

Necklace made of unusual shaped blue glass stones. $75-100. / Brooch made of gilded brass and imitation lapis stones, circa 1910-1920. $65-85.

Brass and Bohemian glass *sautoir*, 20 inches long, circa 1910-1915. $125-175.

Pendant necklace made of brass, simulated star sapphire, smaller blue glass accents and enamel ornamentation, circa 1915. $100-135.

Three pairs of screw-type earrings made of Czechoslovakian glass, circa 1920s. $45-65 each.

Brooch in gilded brass and amethyst-colored stones, marked Czechoslovakia, circa 1920. $75-90.

Bohemian glass and brass pendant necklace, circa 1915. $85-120.

Pendant necklace of brass, enamel and marbleized Catalin, circa 1930. $70-90. / Pendant necklace made of brass and green glass, circa 1910-1920. $75-95.

Necklaces, brooches and hat ornament made of base metals, yellow glass and plastic, circa 1920-1935. $25-75 each.

Three bracelets made of brass and set with yellow glass stones cut *en cabochon,* circa 1915-1925. $50-75 each.

Two Czechoslovakian necklaces made of base metals and imitation turquoise stones, circa 1920-1930. $65-95 each.

Necklace of white base metal and molded glass, circa 1925. $75-95.

Oval brooch of sterling silver with genuine butterfly wing mounted under glass, circa 1905-1910. $80-100. / Geometric link bracelet made of sterling silver with butterfly wings mounted under glass panels, marked Made in England, circa 1920. $75-125. / Sterling and butterfly wing pendant marked Morpho, circa 1920. $65-85.

Molded blue glass necklace marked Czechoslovakia, circa 1930. $65-85.

Two brass and glass necklaces marked Czechoslovakia, circa 1930. $65-95 each.

Triangular pink glass drop with filigree ornamentation and cut glass beads on chain, circa 1930. / Brass and pink glass necklace made in Czechoslovakia, circa 1920. / Pink glass beaded necklace with brass finding, circa 1930. $100-150 each.

Bracelet and matching pin made of enameled brass filigree and simulated carnelian stones, marked Made in Czechoslovakia, circa 1920-1925. $100-150 set.

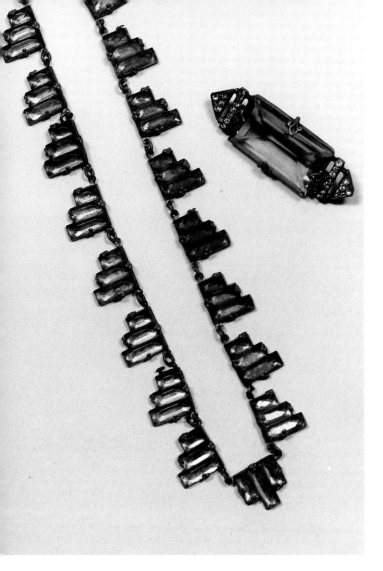

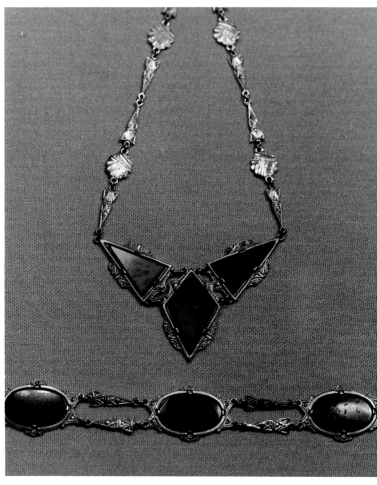

Geometric link necklace made of brass and topaz-colored baguettes in stepped pattern. $95-130. / Brooch made of topaz-colored glass stone and *pavé* rhinestones, circa 1925-1930. $45-65.

Necklace and bracelet in chromium-finished base metal set with simulated lapis stones marked Germany, circa 1930-1935. $150-200 set.

Link bracelet of brass and enamel and cabochon-cut green glass stones. / Sterling link bracelet set with simulated lapis stones, circa 1930. $75-125 each.

Chapter Five

Art Deco

The term *Art Deco* was applied in the mid-1960s to the artistic style derived from *L'Exposition Internationale des Arts Decoratifs et Industriels Modernes,* an international display of modern decorative arts held in Paris in 1925. This exhibit, originally planned for 1916, was postponed because of World War I, rescheduled two more times and finally held in 1925. By the time the exhibit actually took place, the new style was almost fully developed. Over 400 jewelry firms participated in the exhibition. The firm of Cartier displayed over 150 pieces of jewelry which would influence many others in the years to follow.

Sources

The roots of the Art Deco movement go back much further than the 1925 Paris exhibition. Traces of this style, characterized by geometric figures and symmetrical form, could be seen in the work of a group of designers of the Vienna Secession as early as 1903. The geometric style was seen in the works of Josef Hoffman and Koloman Moser of the *Wiener Werkstatte.* The

Pendant necklace made of gilt over brass, large green glass stone and metal fringe in stepped-pattern, made in Germany, circa 1925-1930. $250-300.

rise of the German Bauhaus (Art and Design Institute) in 1919 was also instrumental in influencing the designers in this new and exciting movement of the decorative arts. The most dramatic influence of all, however, came in 1909 when the *Ballets Russes*, directed by Serge Diaghilev, premiered in Paris. The Oriental sets and costumes designed by Leon Bakst incorporated bold colors into exotic fashions and feathered head ornaments. Undoubtedly, the roots of this movement were established before World War I and the style blossomed enormously by the time the war was over. It was an expression of modern times. New and young innovators along with already established jewelers needed a change. They became somewhat intolerant of the excessive use of curvilinear lines resulting in flowing hair and intertwining vines of the Art Nouveau period. A more stylized, abstract and modern approach seemed necessary.

Necklace displaying a striking geometric pattern made of brass and enamel. $125-150. / A popular Art Deco motif of a woman with a wolfhound made in brass and enamel, circa 1930s. $85-125.

Flexible geometric link collar and matching bracelet in chrome and enamel marked Garantie, German, circa 1925. *Heidi Peinsipp Tomasello.* $150-200.

Necklace made of clear square-cut and black rectangular-cut glass stones producing a striking black and white effect, circa 1925-1930. $100-125.

created by ARMBRUST . . . . •
COSTUME JEWELRY

SMART · · · · MODERN · · · INTERESTING

*Be prepared for
Fall demand.
Write your
Wholesaler*

*Sold only
through the
Wholesale
Trade*

*Write today for selection, giving the name of whole-
sale house through which goods should be billed.*

THE ARMBRUST CHAIN CO.
PROVIDENCE
R. I.

H. D. SEEBECK, *Chicago Rep.*
1108 Heyworth Bldg., Chicago, Ill.

H. A. SAUNDERS, *Pacific Coast Rep.*
424 So. Broadway, Los Angeles, Cal.

Costume jewelry with geometric characteristics made by Armbrust of Providence, Rhode Island in 1929.

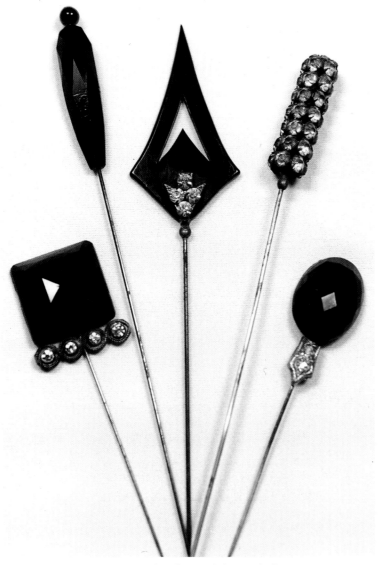

Hatpins made of French jet, Bakelite and rhinestones from 1900 to 1925. $40-75 each.

Brooch made of chrome, brass and enamel in stepped-pattern, circa 1930s. $45-65.

Brooch made of molded glass with gold and silver overlay set in brass, marked Czechoslovakia, circa 1920-1925. $45-65.

Brooch made of silver gilt mounted with amber-colored glass and marcasite accents, marked Czechoslovakia, circa 1920. $50-75.

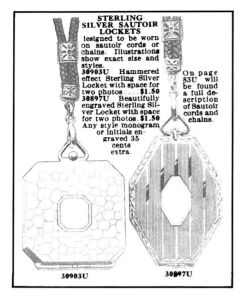

STERLING
SILVER SAUTOIR
LOCKETS
designed to be worn
on sautoir cords or
chains. Illustrations
show exact size and
styles.
30903U Hammered
effect Sterling Silver
Locket with space for
two photos....**$1.50**
30897U Beautifully
engraved Sterling Sil-
ver Locket with space
for two photos. **$1.50**
Any style monogram
or initials en-
graved 35
cents
extra.

On page
83U will
be found
a full de-
scription
of Sautoir
cords and
chains.

Jason Weiler & sons cata-
logue, circa 1927.

Pendant necklace with large red glass
stone suspended from a brass chain. /
Bracelet made of brass with enamel
decoration and large opaque red glass
stone mounted in center. / Pendant
made of brass, glass and enamel, circa
1920-1930. $65-95 each.

Lavaliere made of sterling silver and
marcasites, French, circa 1925. $125-
175.

Necklace of brass and molded red
glass stones. / Necklace made of silver gilt and red glass stones, circa
1925. $75-125 each.

Cartier-style dress clip made of sterling silver, made to look like carved emeralds, rubies and sapphires, circa 1930s. $50-75.

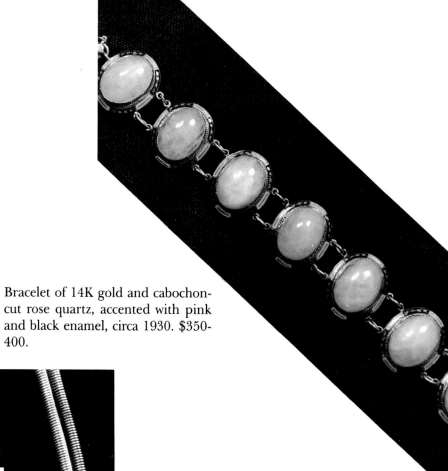

Bracelet of 14K gold and cabochon-cut rose quartz, accented with pink and black enamel, circa 1930. $350-400.

Chrome and Bakelite necklace marked Made in Germany, circa 1930s. *Heidi Peinsipp Tomasello.* $70-90.

Brooch made of chrome and green glass, circa 1935. $65-80.

Choker made of enameled mesh and chrome, German, circa 1930s. $60-85.

Geometric brooch made of oxidized brass set with colored rhinestones, circa 1930. $45-65.

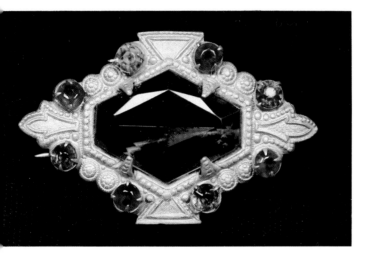

Brooch made of white base metal accented with rhinestones and large oval-shaped green glass stone, circa 1930s. $45-65.

Chrome and glass pendant necklace, circa 1930s. $95-140.

Black Bakelite and chrome-finished pendant necklace marked Germany. / Blue glass and chrome pendant necklace with enamel ornamentation suspended from twisted metal chain, marked Czechoslovakia, circa 1935. $125-175 each.

Two link bracelets made of white base metal and green glass stones, circa 1930. $60-85 each.

Three necklaces made of molded glass with enamel ornamentation, circa 1930-1935. $75-125 each.

Necklace in silver gilt and imitation carnelian. / Necklace in silver gilt and imitation sardonyx made in Czechoslovakia, circa 1925-1930. $95-135 each.

Hat ornament and lapel pin in white base metal set with rhinestones and blue glass stones, circa 1930s. $60-85 each.

EVANS

P1700—Stone set brooch pin with genuine Viennese enamel border, safety catch, non-tarnishing green gold finish. $2.25 ea.

E1700—Pendant ear drops, contrasting stone set, with genuine Viennese enamel border, non-tarnishing green gold finish. $3.75 pr.

E1700—Pendant ear drops, contrasting stone set, with genuine Viennese enamel border, non-tarnishing green gold finish. $3.75 pr.

N1700—Pendant necklace, contrasting colored stones with genuine Viennese enamel borders, safety barrel clasp, non-tarnishing green gold finish $9.00 ea.

N1702—Pendant style necklace in genuine contrasting Viennese enamel with contrasting stones, enamel link chain, safety barrel clasp, non-tarnishing green gold finish.............$9.00 ea.

N1703—Pendant style necklace, contrasting genuine Viennese enamel with stones, safety barrel clasp, non-tarnishing green gold finish.............$6.00 ea.

N1701—Pendant necklace, genuine Viennese enamel and border set with genuine Marcasite, enameled link chain, safety barrel clasp, non-tarnishing Chromium finish. $15.00 ea.

N1704—Pendant style necklace in genuine Viennese enamel, Japanese design with stones, safety barrel clasp, non-tarnishing green gold finish.............$6.00 ea.

N1705—Pendant style necklace in genuine Viennese Jade enamel, harmonizing stones, with enamel links, safety barrel clasp, non-tarnishing green gold finish. $9.00 ea.

B1700—Bracelet set with contrasting stones with genuine Viennese enamel border, non-tarnishing green gold finish..$9.00 ea.

Illustrations three-fourth size.

The LINE with the STERLING TOUCH

Opposite:
Enameled jewelry by Evans Case Company in 1929.

Pendant necklace made of chromium-plated brass, Viennese enamel and set with yellow glass stones, circa 1929-1932. $125-150.

Other influences that played an important role in the Art Deco movement were Oriental, Indian and African art. Creative use of exotic materials such as ivory, jade, cinnabar, mother of pearl, ebony, obsidian and lacquer created modern interpretations of traditional Oriental motifs. The ziggurat or stepped Aztec temples of South America possessed the right geometric look that architects and designers used and modified. African tribal masks became motifs used for designing brooches, earrings and pendants. Reaching into the realms of other cultures was a good source of inspiration. Artistic influences such as Cubism, Futurism and Expressionism enriched the design concept of the Art Deco period. Curves transformed themselves into angles; sensuous women turned into sleek dancers; geometric shapes dominated the designs. Jewelry was adorned with colored enamel in geometric patterns. Bold and striking color combinations such as red and black were used frequently throughout the period. Onyx and diamonds, producing a black and white look, took the forms of bar pins, rings and pendants. This was a very fashionable look that surfaced in the second decade of the twentieth century. The same effect could also be achieved by using materials such as ivory and ebony, ivory and onyx, onyx and mother of pearl, and imitation onyx and rhinestones. Bone along with ivory was artistically carved into brooches, dress clips, buckles, earrings and beaded necklaces. Plastics and glass could be molded or pressed to produce similar effects.

Geometric link necklace show in Lane Bryant Spring and Summer Catalog of 1929.

Necklace of silver gilt and simulated chrysoprase. $85-125. / Geometric link bracelet of sterling and chrysoprase. $150-200./ Brooch made of sterling and chrysoprase, circa 1925-1930. $75-100.

Mexican Art Deco jewelry in silver and dyed onyx displaying abstract tribal mask motifs, circa 1930-1940. $95-185 each.

Two necklaces and a bracelet made of inlaid turquoise marked India, circa 1930s. $100-200 each.

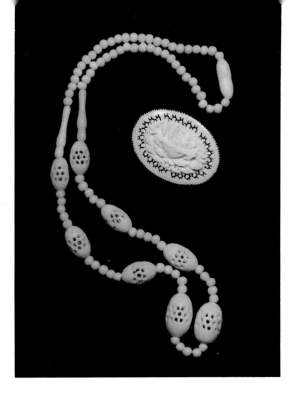

Carved ivory necklace and brooch, circa 1920s. Necklace, $150-185. Brooch, $80-110.

Two brooches made of carved bone, $45-75 each. / Necklace made of carved bone beads, $70-90. / Rose pendant and rose dress clip made of carved ivory, circa 1920-1930. $65-90.

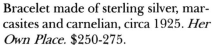

Bracelet made of sterling silver, marcasites and carnelian, circa 1925. *Her Own Place.* $250-275.

Wide silver bracelet with scrolling filigree work, set with chrysoprase stones. / Bracelet in openwork pattern, set with green onyx, marked Sterling 925 Mexico, circa 1930s. $125-175 each.

Settings

The way that stones were set in the modern movement differed from those of previous decades. To create the illusion of total brilliance, stones, especially diamonds for the rich and rhinestones for the less affluent, were *pavé*-set. Much of the ornamental nature of the setting in which the stones had been previously mounted had disappeared. Brooches, necklaces, bracelets and earrings became glittering examples of *pavé*-set stones. The baguette, which was a new rectilinear style of cutting gemstones, also evolved at this time.

Pendant necklace, rhodium-plated, and set with *pavé* rhinestones, circa 1940s. $100-135.

Pendant necklace of Bakelite and brass, Egyptian influence, circa 1925. $100-150.

Flexible bracelets made of aluminum and white base metals, set with rhinestones and imitation emeralds, circa 1920s. The bracelet at the top is made of aluminum and marked Patria Pat. Jan. 29, 1924. $75-125 each.

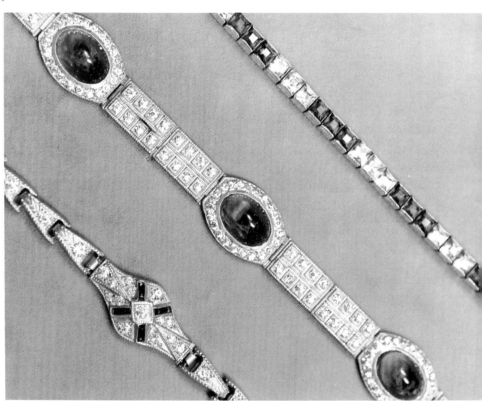

Egyptian

In 1922, archaeologist Howard Carter, after many years of excavations, discovered the tomb of King Tutankhamen. The resulting Egyptian influence had a monumental impact on jewelry and accessories that were produced at this time. Scarabs, pyramids, obelisks, sphinxes and hieroglyphics were popular motifs incorporated in design. Large jeweled collars and bib-type necklaces were fashionable and their popularity continued well into the 1930s. *Cloisonné*, which was an ancient enameling technique, was favored in this period. Lapis lazuli, coral and turquoise were a few of the necessary semiprecious stones used to create the Egyptian look. This influence remained stylish until World War II.

Link bracelet, silver gilt with Egyptian influence, circa 1925-1930. $150-180.

Bracelet and earrings in gilded brass with Egyptian motifs, circa 1930s. $65-80.

Brooch and earrings made of oxidized brass and simulated carnelian, Egyptian influence, circa 1930. $70-90 set.

Necklace of brass and simulated lapis, Egyptian influence, circa 1925. $75-95.

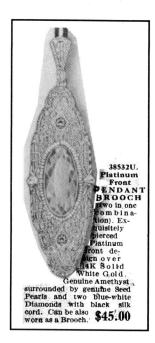

Filigree pendant necklace of 14K white gold, camphor glass and diamond, circa 1925-1930. $250-300.

Choker made of simulated topaz stones set in engraved sterling links. $150-175. / Geometric link bracelet in chrome, glass and enamel, circa 1925-1935. $90-130.

Early Art Deco filigree choker made of chromium-plated base metal and imitation topaz stones, circa 1910-1920. $200-225.

Jason Weiler & Sons catalogue, circa 1927.

Streamlined

The 1920s was a fast-paced society of go-getters and trend-setters. The cloche hats and flapper dresses of the "Roaring Twenties" were a dramatic change from the crinolines and bustles of the Victorian period and the corsets and petticoats of the Edwardian period. Jewelry also changed to fit the fashion picture. Traditional jewelry became a thing of the past. New and different modes of transportation inspired "streamlined" designs in architecture, furniture, glassware, textiles and jewelry. This look, which was called *Art Moderne* at the time, flourished in the 1930s and the 1940s.

Filigree

One style of jewelry closely associated with the early twentieth century and Art Deco period is filigree. This intricate style of lacy, openwork design was all the rage in the teens, 1920s and 1930s. Necklaces, pendants, rings, bracelets and bar pins were exquisitely fashioned from platinum, white gold and sterling silver. In 1919, Benj. Allen and Co. of Chicago advertised sterling silver filigree bar pins with "Platinol Plate" to prevent tarnishing. These pins were set with brilliants and sold for $1.70 to $30.00 each, depending on the detail and workmanship involved. Platinum front bar pins and bracelets in lovely openwork patterns were also offered for sale from Allsop & Allsop in Newark, New Jersey to those who appreciated "jewelry of distinctive design," but were "unable to pay fancy prices."

Trio of chromium-finished filigree pendant necklaces set with cut glass stones and faceted glass beads on silver chains, circa 1915-1925. $125-175 each.

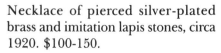

Necklace of pierced silver-plated brass and imitation lapis stones, circa 1920. $100-150.

Pendant necklace and segmented bracelet both finished in rhodium and set with blue glass stones, circa 1940s. $75-100 each.

Four filigree pins with bow-knot ornamentation made of sterling silver and 14K white gold, circa 1920-1930. Sterling silver $50-75 each. 14K, $125-150 each.

Filigree necklace in chromium plate with three rectangular opaque blue glass stones, circa 1928-1932. $100-135.

Sterling filigree pendant necklace set with clear rhinestone and imitation emeralds on chain, circa 1930-1935. $75-95.

Two filigree pendant necklaces made of chromium plate and glass stones, circa 1930s. $75-100 each.

Three completely different styles of filigree necklaces, all chromium-finished and set with blue glass stones, circa 1920-1930. $100-200 each.

High school pendant necklace in silver filigree and mother of pearl, circa 1930s. $65-90.

37325U Brooch or Shoulder Pin, Sterling Silver, open filigree work, set with a small artificial amethyst **75c**

Circa 1927.

Pair of oval sterling silver filigree pins with bow-knot ornamentation set with brilliants, circa 1920-1925. $100-150 set.

38460 32.50   38461 27.00   38462 15.00

DIAMOND MOUNTED PENDANTS
Illustrations show actual sizes. Each Pendant comes complete with a 15 inch neck chain.
38460U 14K Solid White Gold Pendant, mounted with a perfectly cut Diamond and four genuine Aquamarines of fine color and brilliancy..**$32.50**
38461U Platinum Pendant backed with 14K Solid White Gold in a delicate open work design, mounted with a perfectly cut blue-white Diamond and two synthetic Blue Sapphires............................**$27.00**
38462U Platinum Front Pendant backed with 14K Solid White Gold in a pierced design, mounted with a perfectly cut blue-white Diamond..................**$15.00**

Jason Weiler & Sons catalogue, circa 1927.

Necklace made by Walter E. Hayward Co. of Attleboro, Mass. in 1929. The chain used in this piece was a reproduction of the firms original pattern made in the nineteenth century.

Two filigree pendant necklaces made of chromium plate and colored glass stones, circa 1920-1930. $100-135 each.

Pendant necklace of cut glass on chromium link chain, circa 1928-1932. $95-125.

Two sterling silver flexible filigree bracelets, elaborately made, and set with brilliants and synthetic emeralds, circa 1925-1930. $150-200 each.

Filigree and amethyst-colored glass pendant necklace with faceted clear and amethyst-colored glass beads on chain, marked Sterling, circa 1920. $125-175.

Brooch of chromium plate and large bezel-set simulated topaz. $50-75. / Filigree link necklace with alternating topaz-colored glass stones, circa 1930s. $80-100.

Ten different styles of flexible filigree bracelets popular in 1927.

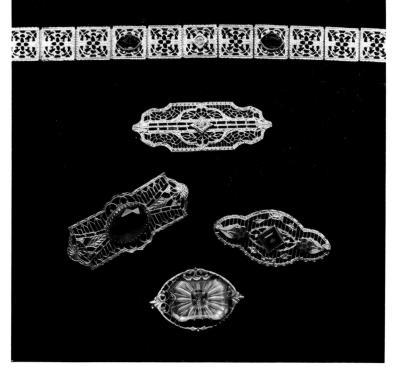

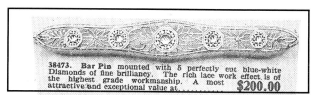

38473. Bar Pin mounted with 5 perfectly cut blue-white Diamonds of fine brilliancy. The rich lace work effect is of the highest grade workmanship. A most attractive and exceptional value at..... **$200.00**

This platinum front bar pin backed with 14K gold retailed for $200 in 1927.

Filigree segmented bracelet finished in chromium and set with imitation stones. $100-135. / Four completely different styles of filigree pins dating from the teens and the early 1920s. $60-85 each.

Filigree pin made of chromium-plated white base metal with rhinestone ornamentation, circa 1925. $60-85.

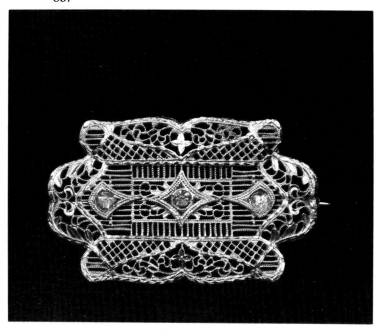

Filigree pendant necklace made of chromium-plated base metal set with large blue glass stone suspended from beaded chain, circa 1920. $125-175.

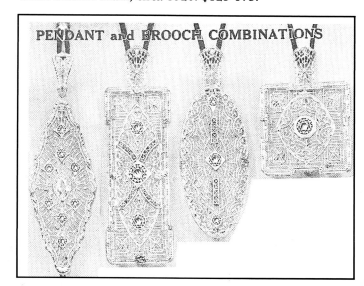

PENDANT and BROOCH COMBINATIONS

These four pendant and brooch combinations made of platinum and 14K gold retailed for $45 to $100 each in 1927.

The PIERCED BRACELET

It's with well founded pride we present our latest line of finely pierced bracelets. Only R. & G. can furnish these lovely, lace-like designs. Like all R. & G. products the workmanship is decidedly superior. Your most exacting trade can be satisfied with these new numbers. Finished in "Nuwite" chromium-plated and set with stones in any of the more desirable colors.

Bracelets

Flexible filigree bracelets with elaborate hand-pierced and engraved work were also set with precious stones, synthetics and rhinestones. Hinged filigree bracelets were very much in demand in the late 1920s and early 1930s. Filigree circle pins sometimes had raised bowknot ornamentation and a real or imitation sapphire, ruby, emerald, amethyst or diamond mounted in the center. This wonderful and delicate jewelry from the early twentieth century is extremely desirable today.

Chromium-plated pierced bracelet made by the R & G Co. Inc. of Attleboro, Mass. in 1929.

Five filigree hinged bracelets, chromium-finished and set with simulated stones. The bracelet in the center is marked Romar Quality, circa 1925-1932. $100-200 each.

Four filigree hinged bracelets with pierced and engraved work, finished in chromium and set with simulated stones, circa 1925-1932. $100-200 each.

In the late 1920s and early 1930s, tarnish-resistant, chromium-plated base metals were used to copy expensive originals. The plating made them look expensive but they were very affordable. Chromium-plated filigree jewelry was often set with real or imitation stones. Frosted rock crystal, sometimes called camphor glass, was mounted in rings, pendants, earrings, and bracelets. A real or imitation diamond was usually set in the center.

Filigree circle pin in sterling silver with bird ornamentation, circa 1925-1928. $45-65.

Filigree pendant necklace of chromium plate set with synthetic sapphires and a brilliant, circa 1920-1925. $90-145.

Filigree bar pin made of chromium plate and set with blue glass stone, circa 1920s. $60-80.

41201U
LADIES' 18K SOLID WHITE GOLD WATCH
Including the 14K Solid White Gold Pierced Bracelet. This fine Watch is mounted with eight perfectly cut blue-white Diamonds and six rectangular synthetic Blue Sapphires. It has a 15 jeweled guaranteed accurate movement. Price of this exquisite combination Diamond Mounted Watch and fine flexible Bracelet (as illustrated) in a handsome presentation **$98.50** box . . . .

38565U
$20.00
Ring 14K Solid White Gold
in a finely pierced and engraved design. Mounted with four perfectly matched, genuine Amethysts and a full cut blue-white Diamond in a pierced setting **$20.00**

Jason Weiler & Sons catalogue, circa 1927.

Rings

Rings were tremendously stylish in the filigree settings. They were made with precious metals and stones in conjunction with less expensive materials. Again they were made to look like the originals. The octagon-style basket setting was popular along with the hexagon domed-top ring. Dinner rings or banquet rings, made with rich lace work were fashioned in various styles, usually set with precious stones. Imitations were made of sterling silver and set with brilliants.

Ring made of sterling silver and synthetic emerald, circa 1930. $100-135.

Filigree ring made of 14K white gold, ruby and diamond, circa 1930. $600-800.

Ring made of 14K white gold filigree, frosted rock crystal and diamond, circa 1930. $275-325.

Ring made of 14K white gold filigree and genuine amethyst, circa 1925-1930. $225-300.

Ring made of black Bakelite and set with rhinestone, circa 1925. $120-150.

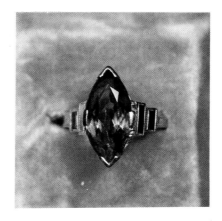

Synthetic sapphire mounted in 14K white gold setting, circa 1930s. $300-400.

38567U   Circa 1927.

$21.**50**

Ladies' Ring 14I Solid White Gold, hand carved and pierced. Mounted with a genuine White Crystal, inlaid with Black Onyx, in the center of which is mounted a perfectly cut blue-white Diamond. A special value at our **$21.50** price of ..

Dinner ring made of 14K yellow gold, platinum and diamonds, circa 1928. This ring belonged to the author's grandmother, Rosann Rickey. $3000-4000.

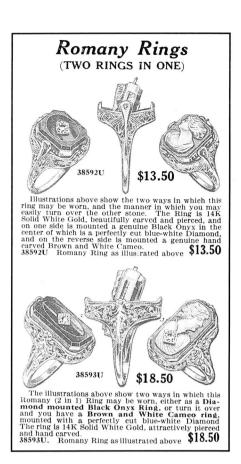

Romany Rings
(TWO RINGS IN ONE)

38592U $13.50

Illustrations above show the two ways in which this ring may be worn, and the manner in which you may easily turn over the other stone. The Ring is 14K Solid White Gold, beautifully carved and pierced, and on one side is mounted a genuine Black Onyx in the center of which is a perfectly cut blue-white Diamond, and on the reverse side is mounted a genuine hand carved Brown and White Cameo.
38592U   Romany Ring as illustrated above   **$13.50**

38593U $18.50

The illustrations above show two ways in which this Romany (2 in 1) Ring may be worn, either as a **Diamond mounted Black Onyx Ring,** or turn it over and you have a **Brown and White Cameo** ring, mounted with a perfectly cut blue-white Diamond The ring is 14K Solid White Gold, attractively pierced and hand carved.
38593U.   Romany Ring as illustrated above   **$18.50**

Romany rings featured in the Jason Weiler & Sons Catalog of 1927.

The Romany ring, consisting of two rings in one, usually had a diamond mounted in black onyx on one side while the flip side displayed a beautiful carved cameo. This type of filigree ring was in vogue in the late 1920s and early 1930s.

Ring made of sterling silver and Fool's Gold, circa 1920s. $100-125.

Sterling rings set with carved and molded glass, circa 1920s. $75-150 each.

Brass ring set with Bohemian glass and accented with colored enamel, circa 1915-1920. $125-175.

Ladies diamond mounted and black onyx rings popular in 1927.

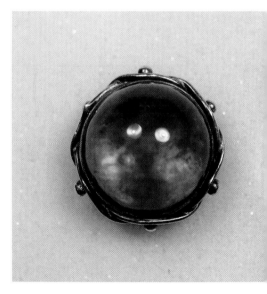

Ring of sterling silver and amber, circa 1930s. $150-225.

Opposite:
Rings made by Stern Manufacturing Company in 1929.

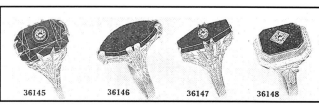

36145   36146   36147   36148

S 200 — $14.50
NUINE CARNELIAN, CHRISTAFRAS
CALSEDNEY — 14K White Gold;
Green Gold Leaves and
meled Ornaments
tion Color Desired

S 208 — $32.75
SYNTHETIC ULTRALITE GENUINE
SEED PEARLS
14K White Gold; Enameled Forget-Me-
Not Flowers in Natural Colors

S 209 — $32.75
SYNTHETIC EMERADA — 14K White Gold;
18K Green Gold Ornaments, Inlaid and Applaid

S 210 — $33.25
SYNTHETIC ZIRCON
14K White Gold; 18K Green Gold
Ornaments, Hand Engraved

S 211 — $24.00
GENUINE TOPAZ — 14K Green Gold; 14K
White Gold Ornaments, Inlaid
and Applaid

S 201 — $33.25
SYNTHETIC ZIRCON
14K White Gold; 18K Green Gold
Ornaments; Enameled Border

S 212 — $21.50
SYNTHETIC ZIRCON
14K White Gold; 18K Green and
Red Gold Ornaments

S 202 — $34.50
SYNTHETIC CEYLON SAPPHIRE
14K White Gold; 18K Green Gold
Ornaments, Inlaid and Applaid

S 213 — $36.00
GENUINE AQUAMARINE
Hand-Engraved Border; 14K White Gold
Forget-Me-Not Flowers Enameled
in Natural Colors

S 203 — $29.50
GENUINE AMETHYST
14K White Gold; 18K Green and
Red Gold Ornaments

S 214 — $32.00
GENUINE AMETHYST
14K White Gold; 18K Green and
Red Gold Ornaments

S 204 — $25.50
SYNTHETIC ZIRCON
14K White Gold; 18K Green and Red
Gold Ornaments, Hand Engraved

STERNSET
Ring Creations

S 216 — $28.00
SYNTHETIC CEYLON SAPPHIRE
14K White Gold, Enameled Shank

S 205 — $25.50
GENUINE AMETHYST
GENUINE SEED PEARLS
14K White Gold
18K Green Gold Ornaments

S 206 — $21.00
ELECTRIC EMERALD
GENUINE SEED PEARLS
14K White Gold
18K Green Gold Ornaments

S 207 — $21.00
SYNTHETIC RUBY
GENUINE SEED PEARLS
14K White Gold
18K Green Gold Ornaments

S 217 — $35.25
FINE BLACK OPAL DOUBLET
GENUINE SEED PEARLS
14K White Gold
18K Green Gold Ornaments

S 218 — $28.75
GENUINE AMETHYST
GENUINE SEED PEARLS
14K White Gold
18K Green Gold Ornaments

*All Sternset Rings are tagged with the metal seal illustrated. The seal is plainly
marked—genuine stone or synthetic stone, whichever the case may be.*

Combination
S 219 — $87.25
FOURTEEN FINE QUALITY
GENUINE AQUAMARINES
TWO 3-Pt. DIAMONDS

14K White Gold
15-Inch Chain

Pendant · · · $51.25
Ring · · · · 36.00

Combination
S 221 — $78.75
SYNTHETIC ZIRCONS
14K White Gold
18K Green and Red Gold Ornaments
15-Inch Chain

Pendant · · · $45.50
Ring · · · · 33.25

Combination
S 222 — $32.75
This Set Comes in
SYNTHETIC RUBY, GENUINE TOPAZ
ELECTRIC EMERALD

14K White Gold, Enameled Border
Mention Color Desired

Pendant · · · $18.35
Ring · · · · 14.40

Combination
S 220 — $55.00
NINE FINE QUALITY
GENUINE AQUAMARINES
TWO 2-Pt. DIAMONDS

14K White Gold
15-Inch Chain

Pendant · · · $29.50
Ring · · · · 25.50

Combination
S 223 — $57.50
SYNTHETIC CEYLON SAPPHIRES
14K White Gold
18K Green and Red Gold Ornaments
15-Inch Chain

Pendant · · · $32.50
Ring · · · · 25.00

Combination
S 224 — $54.25
GENUINE AMETHYSTS and
SEED PEARLS
14K White Gold; 18K Green Gold
Ornaments. 15-inch Chain

Pendant · $28.75   Ring · $25.50

Combination
S 225 — $60.75
GENUINE AMETHYSTS and
SEED PEARLS
14K White Gold; 18K Green Gold
Ornaments. 15-inch Chain

Pendant · $32.00   Ring · $28.75

STERNSET

Ring and Pendant to Match
May be purchased separately or together

Sternset pendants and combinations are
packed in handsome velvet gift boxes and
are particularly effective for display

Order through your wholesaler

Opposite:
Pendant and matching ring sets made by Stern Manufacturing Company in 1929.

Lavaliere of sterling and citrine-colored glass stone, marked Made in Czechoslovakia, circa 1928-1932. $70-95.

Two necklaces of faceted colored glass on fine chains, circa 1930s. $65-85 each.

Three necklaces of faceted glass drops on fine silver chains, circa 1920s. $45-75 each.

Screw-type earrings made of 14K yellow gold, genuine amethysts and seed pearls, circa 1925-1930. $250-300.

Pearls

A "Flapper's" trademark was the pearls she wore to adorn her vampish body. Long ropes of them, measuring up to 60 inches in length, were tremendously stylish in the Roaring Twenties. One strand was "definitely not enough" and so the flapper garnished herself with layers of "faux" pearls. The manufacture of imitation pearls or "indestructible pearls" as they were sometimes called, put a damper on the genuine Oriental pearl market. This new imitation allowed for the masses to indulge in purchasing rather good substitutes for the real thing. Imitation pearls were made in different qualities and some of the best quality imitations were very expensive.

Actress Ina Claire, wearing layers of pearl necklaces and pearl bandeau as seen in *Harper's Bazaar* in 1918.

Deltah Perles by L. Heller & Son, Inc., Paris and New York, circa 1919.

Deltah
PERLES

The final expression of pearl loveliness: rich with the tints and lustre of nature's sea-born gems.

A charming gift - a treasured possession; the last distinguished touch to be added to a woman's costume.

Offered by Jewelers everywhere, whose stocks are of the Heller Quality.

$10 to $300 the necklace. Solid gold and platinum clasps only

L. Heller & Son Inc.
PARIS ☙☞ NEW YORK
Established over a quarter of a century

NECKLACE ZITAH – ONE OF THE DELTAH QUALITIES.

L.Heller and Sons presented a line of indestructible pearls in this period that were given the tradename of "Deltah Perles." They were made in varying qualities ranging in price from $10 to $300. Most of the clasps were made of solid gold or platinum.

Joseph H. Meyer Bros. of New York made the famous "Richelieu Pearls," available in five different qualities and over 1000 styles, lengths and graduations. Clasps were usually of pierced white gold, set with genuine stones.

In 1929, E.F. Higgins Laboratories of Brooklyn, N.Y. announced their line of simulated pearls called "Vesta Pearls." They had a lifetime guarantee never to peel or discolor. The Sears and Roebuck catalog for 1927 offered a line of imitation pearls called "Senorita Pearls" in four different grades marked "A," "B," "C," and "D" luster. The best quality was the "A" luster which in a 36-inch length, sold for $18.45; the "D" luster, in a 60-inch length, sold for 98 cents. Even imitations were imitated.

Mother of pearl

Genuine mother of pearl was also employed and made into beautiful beaded or fringed necklaces, earrings and pendants. The Jason Weiler and Sons Catalog for 1927 stated that their Mother of Pearl came from the Holy Land and that the pearl was gathered from the Red Sea. The choker style necklace sold for $2.50 and a longer strand of graduated mother of pearl beads sold for $5.00. In this same catalog, genuine pink branch coral, in the 54-inch length with a solid gold clasp sold for $4.00 while the 21-inch strand of polished coral beads sold for $5.50.

Two strands of Richelieu pearls with sterling clasps, circa 1940s. $60-85 each.

18-inch strand of polished mother of pearl beads. $50-75. / Brooch made of shells and celluloid links, circa 1925-1935. $40-65.

Two necklaces made of mother of pearl, circa 1930s. $50-75 each.

Beads

Also popular in the 1920s were long strands of cut glass beads in various shapes and in a multitude of different colors. Sometimes these necklaces ended in beaded tassels. They were also worn by flappers so the name "flapper beads" seemed appropriate. Genuine amber beads were still in vogue and they were made smooth or faceted in various shades. The most popular was the faceted and graduated strands of cherry amber. Peking glass beads and colorful Czechoslovakian glass beads were plentiful. Venetian glass beads from Italy also graced this modern movement. Some of these types of glass used in jewelry manufacture is termed "art glass."

Necklace of molded pink glass, rhinestone rondelles and carved Bakelite accent beads with unusual rhinestone clasp, marked France, circa 1925. *Past to Present.* $150-175.

Wonderful assortment of unusual glass beaded necklaces from the 1920s and 1930s. $45-80 each.

Variety of Czechoslovakian and Venetian glass beads, circa 1920-1935. $50-90 each.

Two long crochet ropes of tiny glass beads ending in beaded tassels, circa 1920s. $70-95 each.

Flapper beads made of cut and polished glass beads with beaded tassels, circa 1920s. $90-135 each.

Three strands of cut and pressed glass beads, circa 1920s. $70-95 each.

Black and white geometric glass beads, marked Made in Czechoslovakia. $90-130. / Bakelite hat ornament accented with rhinestones, circa 1930s. $35-50.

Glass beaded necklaces from the 1920s and 1930s, sometimes termed "Art Glass". $75-100 each.

Three crystal and black glass beaded necklaces. The necklace on the left has black enamel work on hexagon-shaped crystal beads, circa 1920s. $80-125 each.

Octagon-shaped topaz-colored glass beads, hand-knotted, 24 inches long, circa 1920s. $100-150.

Five strands of cut and pressed glass beads made in Czechoslovakia from the 1920s and 1930s. $80-150 each.

Two strands of faceted and graduated colored glass beads, circa 1925-1930. $70-110 each.

Pressed glass beads with brass filigree findings, circa 1910-1920. $75-100.

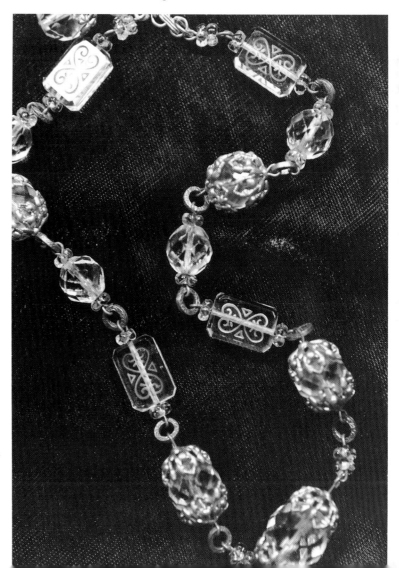

Three beaded necklaces made of cut and polished glass, circa 1920-1930. $60-95 each.
Four strands of Czechoslovakian glass beads, circa 1920s. $60-95 each.

Necklace made of crystal and black glass rings and black faceted glass beads on sterling chain. $100-135. / Black Bakelite bow pin set with rhinestones. $50-75. / Black and white glass Flapper beads, circa 1920s. $75-125.

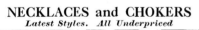

NECKLACES and CHOKERS
Latest Styles. All Underpriced

Genuine stone necklaces and chokers popular in the 1920s.

Pair of rhinestone and green Bakelite pins made in stepped-pattern. $90-110 pr. / Green and clear cut glass Flapper beads. $75-125. / Pair of pins made of white base metal accented with rhinestones and green glass balls suspended from chains, marked Apex Art Nov. Co., circa 1925-1935. $65-95 pr.

Dangle earrings and matching necklace made of cut glass on 14K gold filled chain with gold filled spacer beads and clasp, circa 1930. $150-200.

Czechoslovakian glass beads in topaz color, hand-knotted and graduated, 16 inches long. $95-125. / Brooch with multi-colored faceted glass stones set in filigree setting made of base metal circa 1920-1930. $60-85.

Multi-strand necklace of tri-colored green glass beads with matching earrings, marked Germany. $75-100 set. / Necklace of green glass, seed pearls and enameled chrome, circa 1930-1940. $70-90.

Two fringed necklaces of green glass, marked West Germany, circa 1930. $60-85 each.

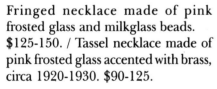

Fringed necklace made of pink frosted glass and milkglass beads. $125-150. / Tassel necklace made of pink frosted glass accented with brass, circa 1920-1930. $90-125.

Necklace and bracelet made of gold-colored balls, Art Moderne style, circa 1930s. $125-150 set.

Fringed necklace and bracelet made of gold electroplate and simulated pearls, marked Coro, circa 1935-1940. $150-175 set.

Coin necklace and bracelet marked Monet Jewelers, circa 1938. $125-175 set.

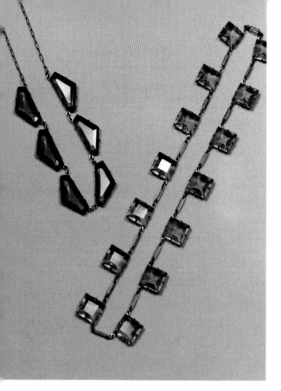

Necklaces, pendants and lavalieres were mass-produced and were still as much favored as in previous periods. The festoon necklace of the Victorian and Edwardian periods adapted nicely to fit into the Art Deco style. Silk ribbons *sautoirs* with attached pendants were worn throughout the late teens and early 1920s. Chains, which were popular in the Victorian and Edwardian periods, were now beginning to disappear. The pocket watch was beginning to be replaced by "Bracelet Watches," or wrist watches. Chatelette watches of the Edwardian era adapted to the Art Deco style and were now called "Lapel Watches." The buckle, which in the previous century was made in one piece, now consisted of two pieces, with a hook on one end and a place to secure the hook on the other. Dress clips, usually sold in pairs, were very stylish in the 1930s. Occasionally, dress clips were sold as sets, with a buckle or a hat ornament to match.

Two geometric link necklaces of blue glass set in white metal frames, circa 1930s. $75-100 each.

Two brass and glass necklaces made in Czechoslovakia, circa 1930s. $75-100 each.

Necklace of faceted blue glass stones set in brass. $90-145. / Abstract floral brooch made of sterling and rock crystal. $100-150. / Necklace of faceted crystal beads set in sterling, circa 1920-1935. $110-160.

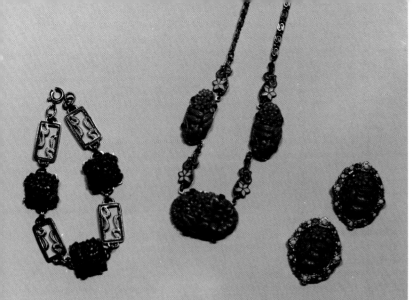

Necklace, bracelet and dress clips of enameled silver gilt and molded glass, circa 1930s. $50-100 each.

Costume jewelry by Stern & Stern Inc., New York in 1929. Noted for reversible Romany rings and creative use of smooth or carved semiprecious stones set in necklaces, bracelets, earrings and rings.

5061

MHILL

Hammered brass pendant set with colored glass stones, circa 1930. $75-95.

Necklace of white base metal and green glass stones, circa 1930s. $75-100.

3042

28-inch strand of blue pressed glass beads and imitation pearls, circa 1930-1935. $100-135.

Two brass and glass fringed necklaces, marked Germany. $75-100 each. Bracelet made of gilded brass and simulated topaz, circa 1930-1935. $70-90.

Blue glass beaded necklace with beaded fringe, circa 1930s. $100-135.

Necklace of brass and glass, unmarked, circa 1935-1940. $175-200.

Enameled brass necklace set with opaque red glass stones, circa 1920s. $90-125.

Two Czechoslovakian brass and glass necklaces, circa 1930s. $100-150 each.

Two topaz-colored glass beaded necklaces with large geometric center stones and brass accents, made in Czechoslovakia, circa 1930s. $110-165 each.

24-inch strand of molded green and orange glass beads with oxidized brass findings. $90-145. / Locket made of brass with green enameled border surrounding green glass intaglio. $85-125. / Brooch of enameled base metal and green glass stones. $50-75. / Brooch of electroplated base metal, enameled petals and leaves, accented with rhinestones. The large flower contains a small receptacle for holding perfume, circa 1920-1935. $80-120.

Large chrome and Bakelite fringed necklace. $200-300. / Three geometric link necklaces made of chrome, circa 1930s. $45-75 each.

Scarab necklace made of semiprecious stones marked 1/20 12K GF, circa 1925-1935. $175-200.

Necklace and bracelet made of clear blown glass balls suspended from brass chain, circa 1930s. $125-150 set.

Necklace made of brass, chrome and copper, circa 1930s. $75-100.

Unusual necklace resembling bunches of grapes made of oxidized silver and large blown glass balls with a pearl finish, circa 1930s. $125-175.

Costume jewelry by Leo Glass advertised in *Vogue* in 1939.

Three fringed necklaces on brass
chains. Top and bottom ornaments
made of plastic; center made of wood,
circa 1930s. $75-125 each.

Necklace made of gilded brass filigree
balls encased at the top with pink plastic drops, circa 1935. $80-120.

Necklace made of seeds and beads on
red cellulose chain, barbaric influence, circa 1930s. $70-90.

Two necklaces made completely of brass, circa 1930s. $65-95 each.

Leaf necklace of gilded brass and polished black Bakelite beads, circa 1930s. $75-100.

Red and blue iridescent blown glass balls on brass neck chain. / Green blown glass balls on cellulose chain, circa 1930s. $70-95 each.

Two pairs of large clips made of white base metal and simulated glass stones, circa 1930s. $85-140 pair.

Two pairs of dress clips made of brass set with simulated emeralds, rubies and sapphires, circa 1930s. $100-150 pair.

Necklace and two brooches made of brass and cranberry-colored glass, circa 1930s. Necklace, $85-125. Brooches, $45-75 each.

Pair of large clips made of white base metal and *pavé* rhinestones, Pat. #1801128, circa 1930s. $75-125 pair.

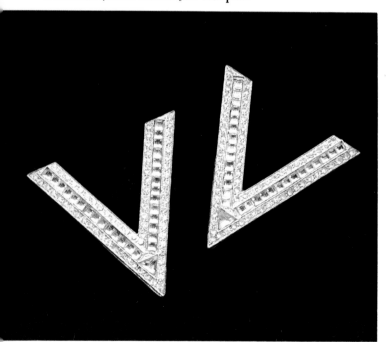

Two pairs of brass dress clips made in the Victorian revival period of the 1930s. $65-95 pair.

Five belt buckles made of base metal and colored glass, marked Czechoslovakia, circa 1930s. $40-65 each.

Matched set consisting of buckle and two clips of white base metal, rhinestones and round blue glass beads, circa 1930s. $140-175 set.

Belt buckle made of base metal with a gold wash and molded plastic flower, marked Japan, circa 1930s. $40-60.

Necklace and bracelet made of green glass beads attached with brass links, circa 1930s. $110-150 set.

Bib necklace of silver and imitation turquoise, circa 1930s. $100-145.

Link necklace with attached initial pendant finished in rhodium. $150-200. / Lapel watch in rhodium set with baguette rhinestones, marked Cyma, circa 1940s. *Marie Rodino.* $350-400.

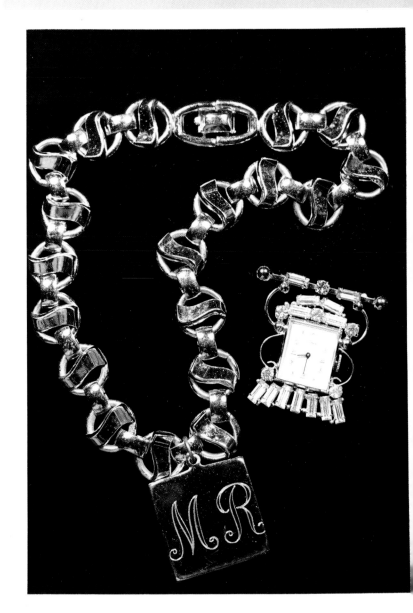

Bracelets

Bracelets came in all shapes and sizes. Any material that could create a new and different look was utilized. Plastics were used, not only because they were less expensive than precious materials, but because they created different looks, colors and textures. Flexible filigree bracelets were popular in the teens and early 1920s. Egyptian influences produced geometric or "slave bracelets" which were worn throughout the 1920s and 1930s. The use of jade, carnelian, sardonyx, amethyst, rose quartz and black onyx created stunning and popular geometric link bracelets with gemstones carved in the style of the Egyptian scarab. Platinum-mounted diamond bracelets were duplicated in sterling silver, aluminum and platinoid and set with rhinestones or rock crystal brilliants.

Link bracelet made of silver gilt in openwork pattern, enamel ornamentation and simulated star sapphires cut *en cabochon,* circa 1930s. $90-125.

Two gold-plated bracelets accented with pearls and rhinestones, marked Reynold & Helene Art Jewelry Company, circa 1940s. This type of jewelry is very similar to that made by Miriam Haskell. $100-150 each.

Bracelet and four small brooches made of base metal and colored glass stones, circa 1920s. Bracelet, $70-90 each. Brooches, $35-50 each.

Bracelet made of gilded brass, enamel ornamentation and bezel-set amethyst-colored glass stones, circa 1930s. $150-200.

Brass geometric link bracelet with alternating simulated carnelian stones. / Large polished brass link bracelet, Art Moderne. / Sterling link bracelet with mother of pearl under glass, circa 1930s. $50-100 each.

Egyptian influences in the 1920s were largely responsible for "Slave" jewelry. This jewelry was offered for sale in 1927 in the Jason Weiler & Sons Catalog.

Flexible rhinestone bracelets and geometric link slave bracelets popular in 1927.

Large enameled brooch and matching bracelet made of electroplated base metal, circa 1930s. $75-100 set.

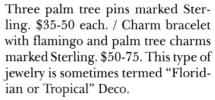

Three palm tree pins marked Sterling. $35-50 each. / Charm bracelet with flamingo and palm tree charms marked Sterling. $50-75. This type of jewelry is sometimes termed "Floridian or Tropical" Deco.

FALL PAYCO-FLEX 1929

Now being shown—
Smart, distinctive
styles, many moder-
ately priced. All in
Sterling Silver.

Lines are unusually
complete this Fall.
A great variety of
clever creations to
select from.

No. 685 Hinged. 3 widths. All colors or combinations in transparent stones only. With or without buckle

No. 1499 Moderne Necklet. Full tint or opaque stones together with baguettes

No. 760 Transparent or opaque stones. Connections of white stones or real marcassites

No. 784 Opaque or transparent stones. Mosaic center or plain

No. B631—3 widths. All colors or combinations in transparent stones only. With or without buckles

Sold Only Thru Wholesalers

H. PAYTON & CO. INC.
PROVIDENCE, R. I.

NEW YORK   CHICAGO   SAN FRANCISCO

Sterling silver and rhinestone jewelry, circa 1929.

Head ornaments

Bobbed hair styles, which appeared about 1917, called for the use of barrettes, bandeaux and aigrettes. A bandeau is a narrow, jeweled band which encircles the forehead. It had been worn in earlier periods but was made popular again in the early twentieth century by Cartier. Some of the bandeaux made by Cartier could be taken apart and made into earrings, bracelets and brooches. Aigrettes, which were typical seventeenth century vertical head ornaments, re-surfaced in the eighteenth and again in the nineteenth centuries. By the 1890s, they became the most prominently-worn head ornament. An aigrette consists of a jeweled ornament supporting a feather. The most popular feathers used were ostrich, the bird of paradise, the Egyptian ibis and the Egyptian white egret, from which the name is derived. In the early twentieth century, particularly in the late teens and early 1920s, aigrettes were again fashionable. However, this time, they were designed with jeweled ornaments resembling feathers and plumes, which were mostly made of diamonds. The less affluent could purchase those made of rhinestones or brilliants. Hair combs had faded out of the fashion picture for a few years when the bobbed hair styles were popular, but in the late 1920s and early 1930s, they were again featured in mail-order catalogs.

France

The Art Deco influence gained so much interest that some prominent French designers of the Art Nouveau period adapted their styles to fit into the more modern movement. Designers such as Lalique and George Fouquet began to design jewelry in the Art Deco style. Prior to the 1925 Paris Exhibition, however, Lalique began designing perfume bottles for Coty and other perfume manufacturers. George Fouquet's son, Jean, also became a noted jewelry designer in this period. Large firms, like Cartier, Boucheron and Van Cleef & Arpels had always been commissioned by wealthy aristocrats, and exquisite designer originals were made from very expensive materials. Smaller firms, such as Trifari and Coro in America copied these designer pieces and made them of less expensive materials. Further down the line, factories copied and adapted these same pieces and mass-produced them, allowing an even broader spectrum of buyers. If this had not been the case, there would not be nearly as much Art Deco costume jewelry available today.

Germany

Not only did the French excel in this movement, but the Germans showed great skill and expertise, producing enormous amounts of geometric costume jewelry. Pforzheim, Germany became the center of mass-produced jewelry in Europe during the Art Deco period.

Jewelry made after the 1925 Paris Exhibition was generally sharper, bolder and more abstract, inspired by Cubism and other art forms. The peak of the Art Deco movement came after 1925. By 1935, the rectilinear form dominated the scene in jewelry, furniture, textiles, architecture, glassware and metalware.

Genuine Lalique beads attached by brass chain, French, circa 1920-1925. *Her Own Place.* $700-800.

Hat ornaments made of white base metal with rhinestone ornamentation, circa 1930s. $30-45 each.

Hat ornaments shown in the 1929 Lane Bryant Catalog.

Hat ornaments made of early plastics with rhinestone ornamentation, circa 1930s. $25-45 each.

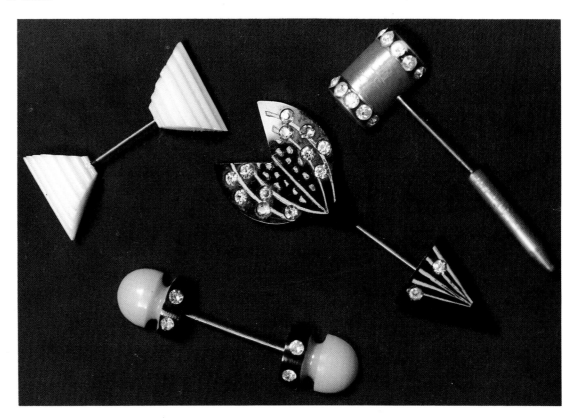

Chapter Six
Other Trends & Influences

By the time the stock market crashed in 1929, bobbed hair styles, cloche hats and unshapely fashions were frowned upon. Paris couturiers, such as Jeanne Lanvin and Jean Patou were creating fashions that were much more elegant than what was seen in the previous decade. Chanel and Schiaparelli continued to make costume jewelry to accent their own fashion creations. Glamorous styles created by Hollywood in the 1930s inspired women to dress in the latest fashions. Just as women of the Edwardian period were influenced by stars of the live stage, women of the 1920s and 1930s were influenced by stars of the movie screen. Fashion catalogs and magazines promoted the glamorous Hollywood look. Greta Garbo, Joan Crawford, Mae West and others were idolized by millions of women. Almost everything that was seen on the "Silver Screen" was copied and mass-produced.

Hat ornaments

From the cloche hats popular in the Roaring Twenties, emerged the sometimes more outlandish 1930s hats. Hat ornaments, extremely popular in this decade, were made of various plastics and inexpensive base metals. Hat ornaments were sometimes adorned with rhinestones. When made of plastic, they were offered in a wide spectrum of colors. The jeweled pin had been introduced in Paris in 1929, but was seen earlier in the United States. It was used for shoulder and sash decoration as well as for hats. The hat ornament was solely a decorative piece of jewelry. It pierced the fabric, creating an illusion of two pins instead of one. The hatpin, on the other hand, was a functional as well as decorative item. Hat ornaments made a very clever fashion statement and became the rage for the whole of the next decade.

The wild and daring mood of the Roaring Twenties virtually came to a halt. What reappeared was a trend for Victoriana. Large floral sprays, flower baskets, girandole brooches, insects and birds were again popular themes. A return to Romanticism was seen in the production of jewelry with classical themes.

Two brooches of base metal and colored glass stones, circa 1930-1935. $60-80 each.

Four Roman mosaic brooches and a bracelet all set in brass, marked Italy, Victorian Revival, circa 1930s. $50-125 each.

Rectangular hand-painted porcelain brooch mounted in a gilded brass frame, marked Limoges. $80-125. / Round porcelain brooch with transferred floral design, circa 1930s. $45-65.

Parure consisting of necklace, bracelet and pierced earrings made of oxidized brass mesh, simulated emeralds, *faux* pearls with *fleur de lis* ornamentation, Victorian Revival, circa 1930s. $125-175 set.

Three floral sprays made of base metal accented with colored glass stones and enamel work, circa 1930s. The center brooch contains a working watch, unmarked. $65-125 each.

Floral spray made of brass wire and simulated moonstones, three-dimensional, circa 1935-1940. $100-150.

Floral spray made of brass wire and multi-colored glass stones, three dimensional, circa 1935-1940. $110-165.

Unusually large floral spray made of silver gilt and blue cut glass drops, three-dimensional, circa 1935-1940. $115-175.

Brass charm necklace, Victorian Revival, circa 1930s. $50-95.

Handmade necklace of red glass stones, circa 1920. $70-90.

Parure made in the Victorian Revival period of the 1930s consisting of a brooch, earrings and brooch/clip combination held together by three chains made of gilded sterling and set with imitation glass stones. $200-250 set.

Girandole brooch of white base metal and multi-colored glass stones, Victorian Revival, circa 1930s. $80-100.

Cameos

Cameos were more popular than they had been for years and were reproduced in many different materials. Plastic cameos were made as well as molded glass cameos. Traditional carved shell cameos were also very stylish and they were set in solid gold, gold filled, sterling silver or base metal frames. Imitation Bohemian garnets were fashionable in addition to French jet and marcasites. Coral, another favorite material of Victorian times, could be easily imitated with plastics.

Cameos popular in 1927.

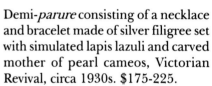

Brooch, in the shape of an insect, made of brass and glass, marked Czechoslovakia, circa 1920. $35-50.

Necklace made of imitation marcasites and mother of pearl, circa 1930s. $40-60.

Demi-*parure* consisting of a necklace and bracelet made of silver filigree set with simulated lapis lazuli and carved mother of pearl cameos, Victorian Revival, circa 1930s. $175-225.

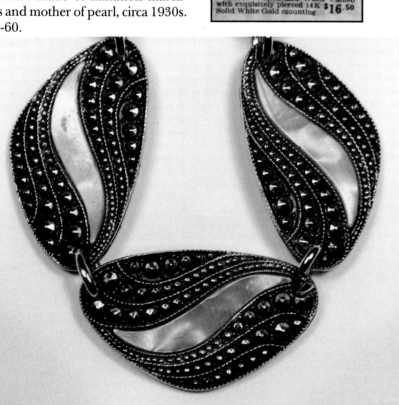

Necklace made of brass and imitation carnelian intaglio, Victorian Revival, circa 1930s. $40-65.

Necklace and matching earrings of marcasites set in sterling silver, marked K.D., circa 1930s. $125-175 set.

Marcasite initial brooch marked Sterling, Pat'd. / Marcasite initial brooch made of plated base metal, circa 1930s. $80-140 each.

Bracelet and matching earrings made of chromium-plated sterling silver set with marcasites, circa 1930s. $150-200 set.

Pair of sterling silver brooches made by Lang, circa 1940s. $75-100 pair.

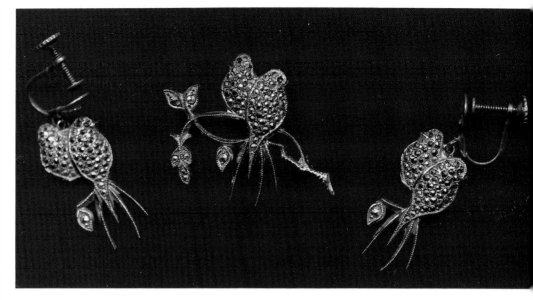

Brooch and matching earrings of sterling and marcasites, circa 1930s. $100-130 set.

Two brooches made of sterling and set with marcasites, marked 925 France, circa 1925-1930. $100-150 each.

Very ornate necklace made of base metal set with an imitation amethyst and emeralds, French Rococo influence, circa 1930s. $125-175.

The French Rococo influence also made a comeback and motifs such as Cupids, crowns and arrows were popular themes for design. Costume jewelry was made to look like real gold and brass was often used to produce this effect. Other base metals were gold plated or gold washed.

Matched set of pins made of white metal and rhinestones, Victorian Revival, circa 1930s. $70-95 pair.

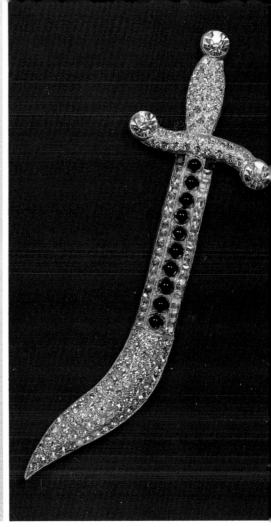

Brooch, in the shape of a sword, made of sterling silver and rhinestones, marked Trifari, circa 1935-1945. $125-175.

Winged knight with enamel and rhinestone ornamentation, marked Sterling, circa 1935-1945. $150-200.

Sword brooch made of aluminum and *pavé* rhinestones, circa 1930s. $100-150.

Opposite:
Parure consisting of necklace, bracelet and brooch made of gilded brass and set with multi-colored glass stones, Victorian Revival, circa 1930s. $275-350 set.

Pendant and hoop earrings made of aluminum and set with rhinestones and imitation emeralds, circa 1930-1935. $135-185 set.

Rhinestones

Just as the Georgians and the Victorians used paste to imitate precious stones, the designers of the Art Deco period used rhinestones (glass imitations of gemstones) for the same reason. The term "rhinestone" derives from early colored glass stones made in the region of the Rhine River of Bohemia. Clear and colored rhinestones, imitating diamonds, sapphires, emeralds and rubies were mounted in all types of jewelry and jeweled accessories. Rhinestone jewelry was made in a variety of styles, materials and price ranges. Rhinestones were set in sterling silver as well as aluminum and other white base metals; sometimes base metals were plated with chromium and later in the period, rhodium, which served as good, non-tarnishable substances. Both chromium and rhodium belong to the platinum family. With the many new advances in technology associated with electroplating since its conception in the nineteenth century, plating became much easier. Using these elements, resembling platinum, gave the jewelry an expensive appearance without the matching price tag.

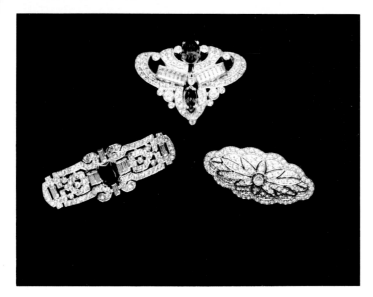

Clip and two brooches of white metal and rhinestones, circa 1935. The brooch on the left is marked Trifari. $75-150 each.

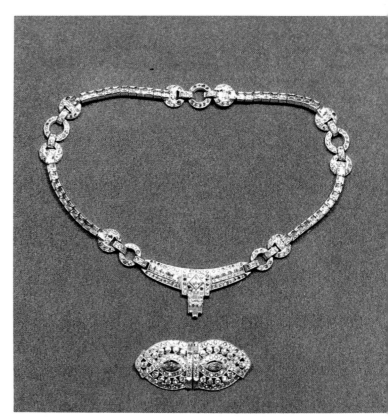

Necklace of chromium-finished base metal and rhinestones. $150-200. / Brooch/clip combination in chromium-finished base metal and rhinestones marked Coro Duette, circa 1930-1935. $125-175.

Gold electroplated necklace set with rows of baguette rhinestones, marked Corocraft, circa 1940s. $175-225.

Three segmented bracelets set with *pavé* rhinestones, circa 1930s. $75-200 each.

When the basic black dress became acceptable for day or evening wear in the 1920s, rhinestone jewelry became the accessory women wanted to wear. Couture originals were made in addition to mass-produced reproductions. As in the first decade of the new century, fashion designers worked hand-in-hand with jewelry designers. Famous couturiers such as Coco Chanel and Elsa Schiaparelli even created costume jewelry to complement their own fashion designs.

Eisenberg

One of the most sought-after types of rhinestone jewelry from this period is that made by Jonas Eisenberg. In 1880, Austrian immigrant Jonas Eisenberg, founded a women's garment company in Chicago. By 1914, the firm called Eisenberg and Sons Originals, was unusual in the sense that the women's clothing they sold was adorned with beautiful jeweled brooches and buttons. These ornaments were so lovely and so desirable that they were found missing from some of the garments in the department stores. Advice from others prompted Eisenberg to market his jewelry separately. Taking their advice, he became very successful. The excellent quality of the rhinestones is due to the brilliance of the finest Austrian crystal made by D. Swarovski and Company.

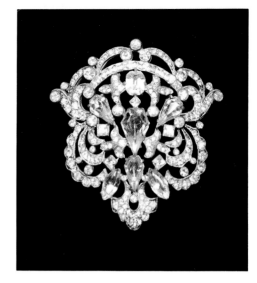

Large rhinestone brooch made of white base metal, Eisenberg Original, circa 1935-1940. $300-400.

Dress clip made of white base metal set with large faceted rhinestones, marked Eisenberg Original, circa 1935-1940. $225-275.

Necklace and matching bracelet of brass and cranberry glass resembling a Hawaiian lei, marked Schiaparelli, circa 1930s. *Past to Present.* $300-400 set.

Hobé

Hobé-made jewelry also ranks high on the list of coveted costume jewelry from the Art Deco period. Filigree, cultured pearls, sterling silver, electrolytic-plating, semiprecious stones as well as beautiful imitation stones were employed to create dynamic pieces of highly fashionable costume jewelry. Hobé wanted to create beautiful jewelry that looked like the real thing but without the expensive price tag. Like Eisenberg, a success story.

Haskell

Miriam Haskell jewelry is noted for its unique use of baroque pearls, glass beads and gold plating to create exceptional examples of costume jewelry made mostly by hand. Early Haskell jewelry, made in the 1930s and 1940s, is rarely signed. The majority of signed pieces came after 1950.

Pendant necklace in the shape of a large flower made of black Bakelite on cellulose link chain. $150-200. / Cameo brooch made of Bakelite, circa 1920s. $95-135.

Necklace, bracelet and earrings made of baroque pearls and rhinestones in ornamental electroplated setting, Miriam Haskell, circa 1940s. $400-500 set.

Necklace and earrings made of Bakelite accented with brass and rhinestones, circa 1920s. $90-130 set.

Plastics

The popularity of synthetic plastics increased throughout the 1920s and the 1930s. Bakelite, the most popular phenolic plastic, could be elaborately carved, as well as cast or molded, into desired shapes. Catalin, Prystal and Marbelette were trade names for other phenolic plastics used to imitate amber and jet. A casein or milk plastic known as Galalith was popular in the early 1920s and was used to imitate tortoise shell, ivory, amber and jade. Plastic jewelry was sometimes set with colored glass stones. After the 1925 Paris Exhibition, noted couturiers, particularly Coco Chanel, designed plastic jewelry set with rhinestones that accented garments she designed for daytime wear. Because Chanel designed and wore them herself, the plastic jewelry industry became big business.

Plastics were so versatile and inexpensive to use that a large percentage of the jewelry manufactured during the Depression was made of Bakelite and Catalin. Plastics came in a wide range of colors, especially the new Catalin of the 1930s. It could also be made transparent, translucent, opaque or even marbleized. Art Deco plastics are extremely collectible today.

Necklace and earrings made of gilt and hand-carved plastic, marked "Leukorite" Germany. $225-275 set.

Bakelite cherry brooch, circa 1930s. $250-300.

Carved Bakelite and French jet beaded necklace. $125-175. / Hand-carved black Bakelite pin. $75-100. / Plastic pin with silver overlay and rhinestone ornamentation, circa 1925. $30-50.

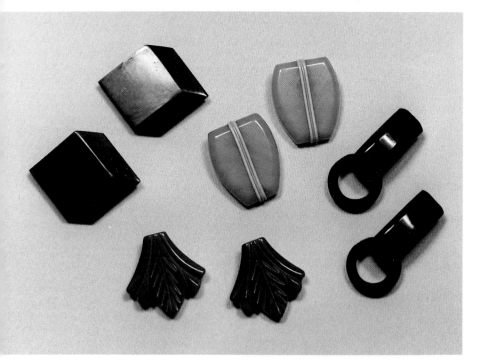

Four pairs of dress clips made of early plastics, circa 1930s. $75-125 pair.

Assortment of Bakelite and Catalin jewelry from the 1930s. $40-95 each.

Basket pin made of molded plastic, circa 1930s. $40-65.

Six carved bangle bracelets made of Bakelite, circa 1930s. $75-150 each.

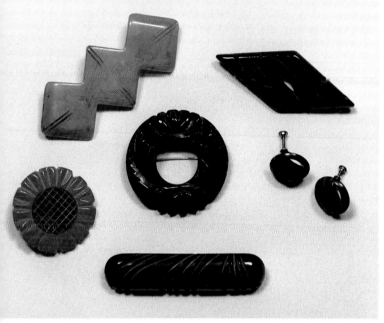

Eight carved Bakelite clips, circa 1930s. $45-100 each.

Leaf necklace made of plastic. $65-90. / Brooch made of Bakelite with gold filled wire spelling "Mother". $45-75. / Necklace made of Bakelite and wood, circa 1930s. $85-135.

Molded plastic pins from the 1940s. $45-75.

Yellow and green flower necklace made of plastic, circa 1930s. $70-95.

Three bracelets made of Marblette, a tradename for a synthetic plastic resin similar to Bakelite. $35-50 each.

Transparent two-piece buckle made of carved green Bakelite with rhinestone ornamentation. / Belt buckle made of genuine amber, circa 1920-1930. $50-100 each.

Brooch made of transparent Bakelite and colored rhinestones, circa 1935-1940. $75-125.

Three carved Bakelite decorative sash buckles, circa 1930. $45-75 each.

Hinged bracelet made of carved Bakelite, circa 1930s. $200-300.

Two-piece buckle with flower motifs under glass and gilded brass frame, marked Made in Czechoslovakia. / Two-piece molded Bakelite buckle, circa 1930s. $40-85 each.

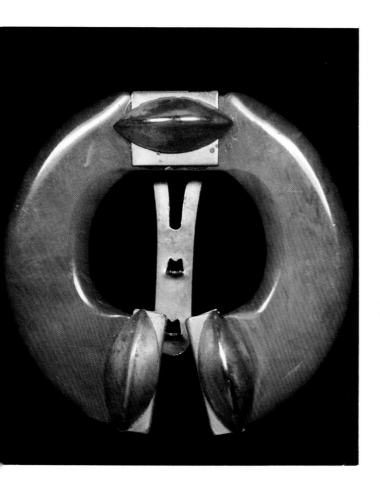

Large clip made of green marbleized Catalin accented with brass, circa 1930s. $85-135.

Even with the scarcity of precious metals during the Great Depression years, jewelry was still abundantly made. Times were hard, but women still needed to feel like women. Manufacturers tried to cater to the needs of everyone. Inexpensive costume jewelry was advertised everywhere. It was sold through mail order catalogs, and in novelty stores as well as large department stores. Because of economic necessity in the 1930s, costume jewelry was accepted by all.

It should be noted that all jewelry produced between 1910 and 1940 is not Art Deco. Some pieces made prior to the 1925 Paris Exhibition are neither abstract nor geometric. Jewelry produced in the teens was delicate but also ornamental. In 1906, aspects of the later Art Deco style could be seen in some of the jewelry designed by Cartier. It has been said that the formation of the German *Werkbund* (German workshops) around 1907 put an end to *Jugendstil*, the Art Nouveau style in Germany. The constant overlapping of curvilinear and rectilinear lines created confusion in separating styles for at least a decade.

Two hinged bracelets and matching earrings made of Bakelite and rhinestones, circa 1930s. $200-300 each set.

Barbaric influences of the 1920s and 1930s intensified the popularity for carved jewelry. Three necklaces and screw-type earrings made of Bakelite and Catalin. Necklaces, $75-100 each. Earrings, $25-40 pair.

TRIFARI, KRUSSMAN & FISHEL • 377 FIFTH AVENUE • NEW YORK

Trifari costume jewelry pictured in *Vogue* in 1938.

ALENÇON SERIES . . . Lace-bosom
dresses bright with jewelled clips, to
frame your head and shoulders in
the flattery of finely corded Alençon
imported from France. Every thread
of the crepe is pure silk, every detail significant of Eisenberg workmanship. Write us for the name of
the outstanding store in your city
where Eisenberg dresses are shown.

Eisenberg & Sons
ORIGINAL

1938 *Vogue* Magazine showing Eisenberg & Sons dresses and jewelry.

Bibliography

Books

Bainbridge, Henry Charles. *Peter Carl Fabergé, His Life and Work*, London, England: Spring Books, 1966.

Baker, Lillian. *Art Nouveau and Art Deco Jewelry*, Paducah, Kentucky: Collector Books, 1981.

———— *100 Years of Collectible Jewelry*, Paducah, Kentucky: Collector Books, 1983.

Bell, Jeanenne. *Answers to Questions About Old Jewelry*, Florence, Alabama: Books Americana Inc., 1985.

Black, J.Anderson. *A History of Jewelry, Five Thousand Years*, New York: Park Lane, 1974.

Ellman, Barbara. *The World of Fashion Jewelry*, Highland Park, Illinois: Aunt Louise Imports, 1986.

Fredgant, Don. *Collecting Art Nouveau*, Florence, Alabama: Books Americana, 1982.

Fusco, Tony. *The Official Identification & Price Guide to Art Deco*, New York: House of Collectibles, 1988.

Garner, Philippe. *The World of Edwardiana*, The Hamlyn Publishing Group Limited, 1974.

Goldemberg, Rose Leiman. *Antique Jewelry: A Practical and Passionate Guide*, New York: Crown Publishers Inc., 1976.

Haertig, Evelyn. *Antique Combs & Purses*, Carmel, California: Gallery Graphics, 1983.

Hendrickson, Robert. *The Grand Emporiums*, New York: Stein & Day, 1979.

Henzel, Sylvia. *Collectible Costume Jewelry with Prices*, Lombard, Illinois: Wallace-Homestead, 1982.

Hillier, Bevis. *The World of Art Deco*, New York: E.P.Dutton, 1971.

Hughes, Graham. *The Art of Jewelry*, New York: The Viking Press, 1972.

Kaplan, Arthur Guy. *The Official Price Guide to Antique Jewelry*, Westminster, Maryland: The House of Collectibles, 1985.

Kelly, Lyngerda, and Nancy Schiffer. *Plastic Jewelry*, West Chester, Pennsylvania: Schiffer Publishing Ltd., 1987.

Koch, Robert. *Tiffany, Rebel in Glass*, New York: Crown Publishers, 1965.

Longford, Elizabeth. *Queen Victoria, Born to Succeed*, New York: Harper & Row, 1964.

Lynnlee, J.L. *All That Glitters*, West Chester, Pennsylvania: Schiffer Publishing Ltd., 1986.

McClinton, Katherine Morrison. *Art Deco, A Guide for Collectors*, New York: Clarkson N. Potter, Inc., 1986.

Mourey, Gabriel, and Aymer Vallance. *Art Nouveau Jewelry & Fans*, New York: Dover Publications Inc., 1973.

Nadelhoffer, Hans. *Cartier Jewelers Extraordinary*, New York: Harry N. Abrams Inc., 1984.

Newman, Harold. *An Illustrated Dictionary of Jewelry*, New York: Thames and Hudson Inc., 1981.

O'Day, Deirdre. *Victorian Jewellery*, London, England: Charles Letts Books Limited, 1982.

Peter, Mary. *Collecting Victorian Jewellery*, New York: Emerson Books, 1971.

Rainwater, Dorothy T. *American Jewelry Manufacturers*, West Chester, Pennsylvania: Schiffer Publishing Ltd., 1988.

Salleé, Lynn. *Old Costume Jewelry 1870-1945*, Florence, Alabama: Books Americana, 1979.

Schiffer, Nancy. *Costume Jewelry, The Fun of Collecting*, West Chester, Pennsylvania: Schiffer Publishing Ltd., 1988.

Shields, Jody. *All That Glitters, The Glory of Costume Jewelry*, New York: Rizzoli International Publications Inc., 1987.

Snell, Doris J. *Antique Jewelry with Prices*, Lombard, Illinois: Wallace-Homestead, 1984.

Snowman, A. Kenneth. *Carl Fabergé, Goldsmith To The Imperial Court of Russia*, New York: Greenwich House, 1983.

Catalogs

BHA Illustrated Catalog of 1895, Schwenksville, Pennsylvania, 1895.

Boston Store Catalog, Fall & Winter 1910/1911, Chicago, Illinois, 1910.

The Crystal Palace Exhibition Illustrated Catalog -London 1851, New York, Dover Publications, Inc., 1970.

Jason Weiler & Sons 52nd Annual Catalog, Boston, Mass., 1927.

John Wanamaker Store & Home Catalog, Summer 1913, Philadelphia, Penna., 1913.

Lane Bryant, Spring & Summer 1929, New York, 1929.

Lyon Brothers Catalog #258, 1899-1900, Chicago, Illinois, 1899.

1922 Montgomery Ward Catalog, Chicago, Illinois, Montgomery Ward & Co., 1922. Montgomery Ward & Co. Catalog and Buyers' Guide, No. 57, Spring & Summer, 1895, New York, Dover Publications, Inc., 1969.

Sears, Roebuck & Co. Catalogs, Chicago & Philadelphia, 1900, 1908, 1909, 1927 & 1930.

Magazines

Delineator magazine (September 1902).

Designer magazine (January 1905).

Ehrichs' Fashion Quarterly (Summer 1879 and 1880).

Godey's Lady's Book (September 1862).

Harper's Bazaar (December 1918).

The *Keystone* (1919 and September 1929).

McCall's Magazine (November 1909, September 1910, and October 1917).

Ridley's Fashion Magazine (1882).

To-Day's Magazine (September 1911).

Vogue (September 1918, January 1938, February 1938 and February 1939).

Index

Other Books by Schiffer Publishing

Handbags Roseann Ettinger. An increasingly popular collector's item, the handbag has been considered a prominent component to fashion for centuries. With hundreds of color photographs, the evolution of handbags, from pouches worn in the Dark Ages to contemporary handbags, is followed. They are discussed by shape, style, material, and designer, with factual text and period advertisements of handbags to pique a reader's curiosity.
Size: 8 1/2" x 11"   Price guide   160 pp.
ISBN:0-88740-372-7   soft cover $29.95

50s Popular Fashions for Men, Women, Boys & Girls; Roseann Ettinger. Those swinging Fifties are fondly remembered in this bright and catchy book of everyday fashions for men, women, boys and girls. A Glossary defines terms as they were used in the Fifties, and the Index will help locate your favorite article.   Price Guide
Size: 8 1/2" x 11"   633 color photos   160 pp.
ISBN: 0-88740-724-2   soft cover $29.95

Compacts and Smoking Accessories Roseann Ettinger. Two of the 20th century's most fascinating fashion influences are highlighted by investigating materials from compact, cigarette case, and lighter manufacturers. With color photographs and advertising pieces arranged chronologically, the book provides a wealth of information in this growing collector's field.
Size: 8 1/2" x 11"   Price guide   160 pp.
ISBN:0-88740-371-9   soft cover $29.95

Forties and Fifties Popular Jewelry; Roseann Ettinger. Thousands of examples of costume and semi-precious jewelry from this era pack these pages in full-color photographs and identifying text. Wonderful advertisments of the period featuring the jewelry add a graphic sense of the clothing styles with which the jewelry was originally worn. The early designers of the jewelry are being recognized for their originality with new materials.
Size: 8 1/2" x 11"   Price Guide   160 pp.
510 color photographs
ISBN: 0-88740-560-6   soft cover $29.95

Baubles, Buttons and Beads: The Heritage of Bohemia Sibylle Jargstorf. This groundbreaking book exposes the jewels, craftsmanship, technological development, and history of Bohemia. Gorgeous color photos show the area's artistry, its most significant designers and manufacturers and their contributions to the art of jewelry, button, and bead making.   Price guide
Size: 8 1/2" x 11"   384 color photographs   176 pp
ISBN: 0-88740-467-7   soft cover $29.95

Jewelry and Metalwork in the Arts and Crafts Tradition Elyse Zorn Karlin. This book provides the best study of Arts and Crafts style jewelry and metalwork to date. The history, characteristics, materials, motifs, influences, and makers' marks are traced. Biographical sketches are provided for the most influential British designers/jewelers/metalworkers. 713 photos, 397 in color.
Size: 8 1/2" x 11"   Price guide   288pp.
ISBN: 0-88740-453-7   hard cover $69.95

Glass Beads From Europe Sibylle Jargstorf. The various worldwide uses of glass beads, from antiquity to the modern time, are presented in this new book, along with the fascinating evolution of the beadmaking industry. Color photographs illustrate the different styles, uses, and patterns of glass beads that originated from or influenced the European industry. Phoenician, Celtic, Viking, Venetian, African, Bavarian, Bohemian, Dutch, French, and Russian styles that were made for symbolic, fashion, magic, and controversial uses are shown.   Price Guide
Size: 8 1/2" X 11"   475 color photographs   160pp.
ISBN: 0-88740-839-7   soft cover $29.95

Costume Jewelers: The Golden Age of Design. Joanne Dubbs Ball. Personal glimpses of that elite core of artists responsible for establishing the costume jewelry industry in the United States. Hundreds of color photographs of their jewelry illustrate the expertise in design and manufacture of such masters as Chanel, Dior, Joseff, Haskell, Boucher, Lane, Trifari, and many more.   Price guide
Size: 8 1/2" x 11"   150 color photos   208 pp.
ISBN: 0-88740-255-0   hard cover $39.95

American Jewelry Manufacturers Dorothy T. Rainwater. Compiled from old trade journals and directories, this is a comprehensive reference of jewelry trademarks and manufacturers and a history of jewelry making in the United States.
Size: 8 1/2" x 11"   thousands of marks   280 pp.
ISBN: 0-88740-120-1   hard cover $45.00

Beads of the World Peter Francis, Jr. Written to encourage collectors and clarify the origins and uses of beads in their native settings, this book is the best and broadest reference available to date. Beads of organic, stone, and glass materials are individually discussed, and certain types of beads are traced to their origins in Europe, the Middle East, India, the Far East, Southeast Asia, North and South America and Africa. 272 color photographs.
Size: 8 1/2" x 11"   Price Guide   144 pp.
ISBN: 0-88740-559-2   soft cover $19.95

The Best of Bakelite And other Plastic Jewelry Dee Battle and Alayne Lesser. This is a treasure chest of Bakelite, Celluloid and Lucite. Layered, carved, molded, translucent, painted and imbedded jewelry styles are displayed in profusion. The captions include the values guide. From common to exceedingly rare, this book presents excitement and the best plastic jewelry to be found.
Size: 11 x 8 1/2"   Value Guide   160pp.
ISBN: 0-88740-901-6   hard cover $39.95

Masterpieces of Costume Jewelry Joanne Dubbs Ball & Dorothy Hehl Torem. This important reference takes an in-depth journey through the phenomenal ascent of costume jewelry through the 20th century. The costume jewelry designers are discussed individually and their work is displayed in hundreds of magnificent photographs of their masterpieces. Unsigned masterpieces are also included.
Size: 8 1/2" x 11"   Price Guide   208pp.
ISBN:0-88740-900-8   Hard cover $49.95